Hastings' Illustrations

ROBERT J. HASTINGS

Broadman Press / Nashville, Tennessee

© 1971 • Broadman Press

All rights reserved

4236–11

ISBN: 0–8054–3611–1

Dewey Decimal Classification Number: 808.88

Library of Congress Catalog Car Number: 74–145982

Printed in the United States of America

5.O7018

Index

(Figures refer to the number printed with each illustration title.)

Other Books by Robert J. Hastings

MY MONEY AND GOD
> (stewardship as related to material posses-
> sions)

A WORD FITLY SPOKEN
> (how to use illustrations in speaking and
> writing)

A CHRISTIAN MAN'S WORLD
> (stewardship of the total life for laymen)

THE CHRISTIAN FAITH AND LIFE
> (a weekday Bible study text for teen-agers)

HOW TO MANAGE YOUR MONEY
> (stewardship of the nine-tenths)

HOW TO LIVE WITH YOURSELF
> (self-help through Christian principles)

TAKE HEAVEN NOW
> (messages on the Beatitudes)

DEVOTIONAL TALKS ON EVERYDAY OBJECTS
> (talks based on object lessons)

Preface

One of my biggest mistakes as a young seminary student was purchasing a new set of a popular multivolume commentary filled with hundreds—maybe thousands—of sermon outlines. My, how impressive they looked on my shelves, their black covers highlighted by gold lettering!

But I later corrected the mistake by selling the whole lot, and I've never regretted it. Why? Because I soon learned that communication is more than quaint outlines and clever alliteration.

The average listener is no more interested in a speaker's outline than he is in the skeleton of a pretty girl.

True, a speaker will organize his material in his own mind, and make some systematic presentation. But his audience will remember the illustrations that illumine his truths far longer than they will the skeleton.

When Johnny's mother, urging him to eat his oatmeal, warns that he's only skin and bones and will never make the football team, that's not a compliment!

Yet many lectures, sermons, speeches, and classroom discussions are nothing more than skin and bones—a few bony sentences tied together with skins of verbal pap.

I smile

I always smile (inside) when a fellow minister remarks, "I've got an outline here that will really preach!" I've never seen an outline yet that will preach or that I would cross the street to hear. I have heard many wonderful messages that overflowed with true-life experiences. But the outline was in the background, the same as the architect's drawings when one is admiring a completed cathedral.

I always cringe when a speaker or teacher tries too hard to outline a book of the New Testament, such as Romans or Revelation. If Paul or John should come back in the flesh and try to understand what they wrote on the basis of some of our artificial outlining, they would be mystified. They wouldn't even recognize what they had written!

Lovers don't bother to "outline" their words of endearment to each other. Billy doesn't use artificial alliteration to describe his first day at school. Then why get in the pulpit or classroom and garble the message with point one, subpoint two, and point three in parentheses? The average person couldn't care less.

One reason is because our generation is geared to television, movies, full-color magazines, and other visual stimuli. Yet the public speaker must often depend on verbal communication alone. He competes with television programs that are episodic in nature, i.e., a series of episodes or dramatic incidents, none of which require prolonged concentration.

Speakers can imitate this technique by using a series of illustrative devices that capture and hold the sustained interest of their audience.

Deaf ears

Remember that before you can persuade a person, or teach him, or lead him to agree with you, you must get his attention. You might offer the most profound truths, but they fall on deaf ears unless you first whet the interest of your listeners.

"But preaching and teaching is more than a string of stories," you object.

This is true. It is entirely possible to entertain a congregation with one story after another, yet never convey basic truths. So we are not talking about storytelling. We are talking about the supportive use of illustrative materials to drive home the basic truths of your message.

First, then, decide on the central truths of your message. (Ideally, this should be one, central idea. A Fuller Brush salesman doesn't try to sell every brush in his case to every housewife he calls on.) In your mind, formulate some systematic method (outline) of presenting that truth. Then look for good supportive illustrations that all age groups can understand.

When you step in the pulpit, clothe your truths in warm, human, believable illustrations from life. You will soon see a difference in how your people listen and respond.

Jesus was a master illustrator. He used illustrations so frequently that Mark testified "without a parable spake he not unto them" (4:34). His skill in their use is proven by the fact that "the common people heard him gladly" (Mark 12:34).

About one fourth of Jesus' words in Mark and one half of those in Luke are in parables. The word *parable* appears about fifty times in the New Testament.

> He spoke of lilies, vines, and corn,
>   The sparrow and the raven;
> And words so natural yet so wise
>   Were on men's hearts engraven.
> And yeast and bread and flax and cloth,
>   And eggs and fish and candles.
> See how the whole familiar world
>   He most divinely handles

"To light up"

The word "illustrate" is from the Latin *illustrare,* which means "to light up." Windows light up a house; pictures light up a newspaper. So illustrations shed light on ideas.

C. H. Spurgeon said that illustrations are windows that let light into the chambers of the mind. He believed that bald statements are soon forgotten but that "an apt illustration sticks in the soul like a hook in a fish's mouth."

Before you catch a fish, you first attract his attention through color or movement of the lure. Fish bite only what they see. People understand only what they can see through the windows of their imagination or experience.

What is an illustration? Frankly, I prefer the term "illustrative material," which includes far more than a story or anecdote. In this larger context, illustrative material includes personal experiences, snatches of poetry, statistics, humor, quotations, proverbs, fables, similes, object lessons, figures of speech, puns, biography, current events, hymn stories, epitaphs, acrostics, legends, drama, art, satire, sports, word pictures, picturesque speech, ad infinitum.

One minister who farmed during the week and preached on Sunday was highly effective despite his lack of formal education. He described his method. "By Monday, I try to select a Scripture that has some meaning for my own life. Then as I go about my work through the week, I look for ideas and illustrations that will help me explain that Scripture on Sunday." Wouldn't you enjoy that kind of preaching, whether that man ever read a sermon outline book, or knew the difference in Roman numeral I, arabic 1, and 1 in parentheses?

Recently a retired minister told me about his first sermon. "I attended church in a schoolhouse in North Dakota. One Sunday our preacher was sick and sent word for me to hold services. I was only seventeen and overwhelmed. He told me to pick a Scripture that was dear to me, and just tell the folks why. I followed his advice and have been doing the same for sixty years."

I sometimes think that we make preaching, speaking, teaching, and writing too hard. In our attempts to be profound, scholarly, and precise, we miss the chance to talk with (not "to") people on the level that has meaning for their everyday lives.

Don't interpret life on Sunday in such a way that it can't be lived on Monday. Good illustrations help bridge the gap between Sunday-go-to-meeting religion and Monday-go-to-work realism.

Sources of illustrations

Where can you find good illustrations? From books such as this one? Perhaps. But your best illustrations come from your own observation. Collections of illustrations, such as this one, should be more suggestive than exhaustive.

If you select your sermon topic, or lesson subject, early in the week (better still, weeks ahead), then illustrative material will break out all around you—on billboards, in conversation, magazines and newspapers, television, the changing seasons, and most of all, from your own experiences. People are more interested in what you have experienced, in what you think, than they are in secondary experiences.

In this book, which I hope is the first of a series, I have selected illustrations from my own life, my sermons, my own books and articles, my reading, my observation. I look first for human interest, for if what you have to say isn't interesting, not many people will listen, regardless of how important it is. (Don't scold an audience for not listening. Make it so interesting they can't help but listen. A single grain of sugar is more appealing than a whole barrel of vinegar.)

To increase human interest, and to illustrate what I mean by the personal element in preaching and teaching I have written this book in the first person.

Those who use the illustrations will, of course, adapt them to his own style.

Let me add ten "don't's":

1. Don't apologize for using illustrations ("You will pardon this illustration, but . . .").

2. Don't apologize for personal experiences ("Forgive me for this personal reference, but . . .").

3. Don't wait until the end of your message to use your illustrations. Better still, start out with one.

4. Avoid such cliches as "I read a story once . . ." or "The story is told that . . . ." Simply tell the story. (Your listeners probably have enough intelligence to know that you read it or heard it somewhere.)

5. Don't betray the confidence of those with whom you have counseled by telling their problems publicly.

6. Don't use the experiences of others as if they happened to you.

7. Don't be afraid to use personal experiences, but avoid ostentation or overuse of such propensities as "my church . . . my deacons . . . my wife . .. my children."

8. Don't be afraid to share your personal failures and fears as well as your glowing success stories. Listeners will more readily identify with speakers who are human rather than porcelain.

9. Don't use illustrations if you doubt they ever really happened.

10. Don't use the same old illustrations over and over. Thin

illustrations, like smoothies and retreads on the highway, may result in a blowout.

The volume

Speakers have a way of turning up the volume when they run out of soap. Some congratulations are weary of noise pollution in the sanctuary. They want sense, not sound. "If the iron be blunt, and he do not whet the edge, then must he put to more strength" (Eccl. 10:10).

So slow down the sound and the fury! Instead, switch to segments of real life. Clothe those teaching outlines with the flesh of believability. Even you will better enjoy what you're saying!

1. A memorable flight plan

At 9:30 P.M. (CST), December 24, 1968, millions of persons, glued to TV and radio, were electrified by a Bible reading from outer space. It was coming from Apollo 8, the first spacecraft to orbit the moon. "Apollo 8 has a message for you," announced commander Frank Borman.

Major Bill Anders began reading, "In the beginning God created the heaven and the earth . . ."

Back on earth, N.B.C.'s David Brinkley said in a reverent comment, "If my memory serves me correctly, he's reading from the first chapter of Genesis."

Captain James A. Lovell, Jr., continued, "And God called the light day . . ."

Col. Borman concluded, "And God said, Let the waters under the heavens be gathered . . ." Then he signed off, "And from the crew of Apollo 8, we pause with good night, good luck, a merry Christmas, and God bless all of you—all of you on the good earth."

Those who heard the live telecast from this first moon-orbiting space probe will never forget how it captured the imagination of the whole world.

Christianity Today compared the event to Samuel F. B. Morse's first wireless message from Numbers 23:23, "What hath God wrought!"

Contrary to popular belief, the astronauts did not read from Bibles, as they would have required fireproof plastic covering and been difficult to get to. So just before launchtime, the three astronauts decided to type the Genesis selection right onto their flame-resistant flight plan.

Frank Borman, a member of St. Christopher's Episcopal Church in Houston, is credited with the idea. Later he joked, "One of the truly historical things was that we got that good Roman Catholic, Bill Anders, to read from the King James Version."

Over 100,000 letters poured into NASA's Houston head-quarters, with praise for the Bible reading running 1,000 to 1.

The New York Board of Rabbis said, "Your reading from Genesis evoked a responsive chord in the hearts of all spiritually attuned people throughout this good earth . . ."

A few verses from Genesis were appropriately typed on the flight plan of Apollo 8. All of the Bible, typed indelibly into our lives, would make a good flight plan for humanity.

2. Over simplification

A fool is a person with short answers to long questions. Anyone is bound to be a quack who says, "This 'ism' is the only disease of mankind, and this pill will cure it." As Benjamin Franklin said, "Half the truth is only a great lie." Oliver Wendell Holmes concluded that "No generalization is worth a damn—including this one."

To simplify is to falsify. No problem in which many strings of action are interwoven can be reduced to just one thread. Cureall pills are peddled by phonies to be swallowed by the unwary. Beware of labels, slogans, half-truths, and oversimplifications, such as:

> Rags make paper.
> Paper makes money.
> Money makes banks.
> Banks make loans.
> Loans make poverty.
> Poverty makes rags.

True, paper is used to make money, but also many other products. True, banks make loans, but they also provide numerous other services. Yes, some loans lead to poverty, but they also lead to wealth when properly used.

A half-truth is often more dangerous than a lie, because it has just enough validity to trick the naive.

3. Building on fear

Although Robert Koch proved to the world that diseases are transmitted by microbes or germs invisible to the human eye, it was the French chemist Louis Pasteur who discovered how to use weakened microbes to inoculate against all kinds of infectious diseases.

His first successes were with anthrax and chicken cholera. Next he turned to a search for the deadly virus of hydrophobia. But before he could develop a serum of weakened hydrophobia microbes, he must first find and isolate the killer virus.

To do this, it was necessary for Pasteur to experiment with dogs that were mad with rabies. In the lab he would stick his beard within inches of their fangs so as to suck froth into glass tubes. Using these specimens, obtained at such risk of life, he hunted the microbe of hydrophobia.

And succeed he did. But the serum had to be proven. The first subject was a nine-year-old boy by the name of Joseph Meister from Alsace. His mother came crying into Pasteur's laboratory, leading her pitiful, whimpering, scared child, hardly able to walk from the fourteen gashes inflicted by a mad dog. "Save my little boy," she begged. It was the night of July 6, 1885, when Joseph became the first recipient of the weakened microbes of hydrophobia in human history. After fourteen inoculations, the boy went home to Alsace and had never a sign of the dreadful disease.

When there were a dozen other serious diseases whose microbes had not yet been found, why did Pasteur risk his life to experiment with the deadly hydrophobia?

The answer may be from his childhood. "I have always been haunted," he said, "by the cries of the victims of a mad wolf that came down the street of our town when I was a little boy."

Sometimes fear paralyzes one into useless inaction. Constructively, fear can goad us into worthwhile action.

4. Not guaranteed

A rabble-rouser once complained to Benjamin Franklin that the United States Constitution is a mockery. "Where is all the happiness it guarantees us? I certainly didn't get my share!"

Franklin replied benignly, "My friend, all the Constitution guarantees you is the pursuit of happiness. You have to catch it for yourself."

5. When life grows empty

An aged and prosperous businessman worried about who would carry on after his death. His only relatives were three young nephews. So he called them in and said that one of them would be his successor. "But I have a problem. And the one who solves it shall inherit my business," he said. "I have here a large room, which I want to fill as soon as possible. Here is a small coin for each of you. Go now, but return at sunset, and see what you can buy with this coin to fill the room."

Hurriedly they went their way to the market, and as twilight fell, they returned. The first youth was dragging a bale of straw. When loosened, it made a pile so great that it filled half the room. He was complimented by the other two as they helped him clear it away.

The second youth brought in two bags of thistledown which, when released, filled two thirds of the room.

Now it was time for the third nephew, who was standing still and forlorn. "And what have you?" asked his rich uncle. "I gave my coin to feed a hungry child," he replied, "leaving only one farthing. With it I bought a flint and this small candle." Using the flint, the third boy made a spark and lit the candle, which filled every corner of the room with light."

Love and light and friendship fill the empty rooms of life as well as refrigerators and stereos and easy chairs.

6. Life without meaning

Without proper punctuation, words can be meaningless. Take these fourteen as an example: that that is is that that is not is not that it it is

Now punctuate them, and they read: That that is, is that that is not. Is not that it? It is.

The significance of the fourteen unpunctuated words is not what they say, but what they don't say. They say nothing because they are not punctuated.

Life is that way. Unpunctuated, it is monotonous and meaningless. It takes the exclamation points, question marks, periods, and the dashes to make life rich and relevant. Life without punctuation is like a piano with only one note, a phone book with one number, a thermostat with one degree, or a highway with one sign.

The question marks of life perplex us, the commas try our patience, and the periods bring rebellion at man's mortality. But otherwise life is only a riddle, a monotonous succession of unbroken days.

7. Overly-optimistic

Optimism is a fine virtue, but even it can be carried too far. Like the fellow who requested that when he died, a U-Haul trailer should be hooked on behind the hearse. He thought he could take it with him!

8. The power of neglect

What is the best way to destroy a garden? You could drown it with too much water, or burn it up with too much fertilizer. You could plow it, chop it, burn it, or pull up all the plants by the roots. But why all the sweat? Just leave it alone, and the weeds and insects will do it for you.

What is the best way to ruin a friendship? You could telephone everyone you know and spread malicious rumors about your friend. You could make false accusations directly to your friend. You could borrow from him and fail to repay. You could write him insulting letters. But why all the sweat? Just leave him alone, and neglect will kill the friendship. Act as if he doesn't exist. Forget his telephone number. Look the other way when you meet him.

What is the best way to destroy a church? You could vandalize the building by breaking the windows, shredding the hymnals, painting obscenities on the walls. You could disrupt the worship services, be rude to visitors, or tell all the leaders what a miserable mess they are making. But why all the sweat? Just live as if your church doesn't exist. Ignore it. Don't go around it. Don't give. Don't visit. That part of the church which is you will gradually die of itself.

What is the best way to destroy your Christian witness? You could throw your Bible in the trash can. You could profane the name of God in your conversation. You could argue against the Christian way of life and everything that Christ and his gospel stands for. But why all the sweat? Just live as if there were no God. Just read other books as if there were no Bible. Forget to pray. Concern yourself only with yourself, and forget such nonessentials as compassion, pity, and concern.

Destructive persons are not necessarily violent. Some are merely neutral—but also quite tasteless.

9. He tried

W. E. Thorn tells about the first little country church he served. After attending many clinics on stewardship, he came to the conclusion that the trouble with his church was that it didn't have a unified budget. So for several Sundays in a row, he preached on "The Unified Budget."

Finally in a church business meeting, one of the deacons asked an embarrassing question. "Pastor, what is a 'unified' budget anyhow?" The young preacher fumbled for words, finally asking for the discussion to be delayed.

That afternoon pastor Thorn asked the treasurer how he handled the finances. "There are two items in our budget," he said, taking two fruit jars down from a shelf. "There is the flower fund and there is the preacher's salary."

Thorn noticed right off that the flower fund was in a quart jar while the pastor's salary was in a pint jar. So with great indignation he said, "We need a *unified* budget."

The treasurer squinted at the young preacher and said, "Okay pastor, if that's the way you want." He then took the pint jar and emptied it into the quart jar.

That was the last time pastor Thorn mentioned a "unified" budget out there!

10. Skimming the surface

Have you ever wondered just how much of the light produced by the sun reaches, or is reflected off of, our earth? The answer will probably surprise you!

Light pours forth from the sun in all directions. Without thinking, we might consider it a flat surface directing its rays solely at the earth. But not so. Light streams from the giant ball of fire which we call our sun in all directions. The result is that *less than one part in half a billion parts* of the sun's radiant energy reaches our earth! For every one ray of sunlight that dances on a June meadow, a half billion rays are dancing somewhere else! Here, then, is an almost inexhaustible source of heat, energy, and light. At the best, we tap an infinitesimal fraction of its potential.

Can we make a similar comparison with God's grace, love, and wisdom? Who can explore it? Who can dare claim he has exhausted God's resources?

"O the depth of the riches both of the wisdom and knowledge

of God! how unsearchable are his judgments, and his ways past finding out!" (Rom. 11:33).

11. The key question

Cowardice asks, "Is it safe?"
Experience asks, "Is it proven?"
Pride asks, "Is it popular?"
Greed asks, "Is it profitable?"
Doubt asks, "Is it practical?"
But conscience asks, "Is it right?"

12. Shut that door

Doors, both literally and figuratively, are prominent in the Bible. After Noah and his family were safely in the ark, "the Lord shut him in" (Gen. 7:16). After Christ left the disciples, and before they experienced new power and courage at Pentecost, they met "when the doors were shut . . . for fear of the Jews" (John 20:19). The five foolish virgins who went for extra oil found on their return that the door to the marriage feast was shut (Matt. 25:10). Jesus said, "I am the door: by me if any man enter in, he shall be saved" (John 10:9). And in Revelation 3:20 he said, "Behold, I stand at the door, and knock."

Every Christian should close at least two doors. First, he should close the door to the past and major instead on the present. Paul wrote about "forgetting those things which are behind" (Phil. 3:13). So long as we keep yesterday's door ajar, even slightly, we are tempted to waste our energies on mistakes of the past. To keep yesterday's door open is like burying the hatchet only to return the next morning to dig it up!

Second, he should close the door to outside interferences when he prays. "But thou, when thou prayest, enter into thy closet, and when thou hast shut thy door, pray to thy Father which is in secret" (Matt. 6:6). This does not mean that God is deaf to prayers offered while we work, or drive down the highway, or watch television. It does mean that unless we seek the secret place, the noise of our environment is liable to distract our attention. God can hear above the bedlam, but can we intelligently verbalize our prayers when surrounded by noise? Sometimes, yes. But those who are most effective in prayer testify to the value of the secret place, at least occasionally. No, this does not always mean shutting a literal door of wood or glass or steel. It does mean shutting the doors of our minds to whatever distracts.

It is good to open the door for a breath of fresh air or to open a door to new opportunities. It is equally good to *close* some doors.

13. Preoccupation

Maybe we had never thought of utilizing nursery rhymes as sermon illustrations. But there are some real possibilities for the preacher with imagination. Take this one for example:

> Pussy Cat, Pussy Cat, Where have you been?
> I've been to London town to see the queen.
> Pussy Cat, Pussy Cat, What did you there?
> I chased a little mouse under her chair.

The point is that there were many things to do and see in the big city of London. But this cat did what she could have done in any barn—chased a mouse under a chair. The illustrative power rests in this comparison. Some of us go through life dealing with mere trivialities when we could be moving mountains. We are content to idle the days by, never measuring up to the full measure of our potential. And is there any greater loss than to live three score and ten and never accomplish that for which one has every potential and opportunity?

14. True religion

A psychologist once interviewed 142 ministers, rabbis, and priests in search of an answer to the question, "What does it mean to be religious?" He reports five basic concepts that these men have. First, those who major on creeds, ritual, and tradition (the formalists). Secondly, those who magnify a negative morality, i.e., don't drink, smoke, gamble, etc. (the puritanical). Third, the humanists, who stress brotherhood of all mankind and social programs to solve current problems. Fourth, those who magnify faith in God. And fifth, the group which emphasizes church activities and obedience to laws and commandments.

Personally, we like Micah's definition of true religion. It is hard to improve on. "He hath shewed thee, O man, what is good; and what doth the Lord require of thee, but to do justly, and to love mercy, and to walk humbly with thy God?" (Mic. 6:8).

15. "God didn't hear us"

In May of 1970, a disastrous earthquake shook Peru, killing as many as 50,000 people, many of whom were buried under a mass of mud and rocks falling from the Andes Mountains. The number of the dead was so great that many were buried in trenches, wrapped in blankets, and many children in old newspapers. Lamberto Guzman, a journalist in the city of Yungay, said men and women were holding hands in groups, shouting to God to have compassion. Then he added, "God didn't hear us. The earth kept trembling."

Novelist James L. Johnson tells how he and his eight-year-old boy were watching a TV documentary about people living in tin shacks in Saigon, dying of meningitis because the available penicillin had been siphoned into the black market. Turning to his father with tears in his eyes, the eight-year-old asked, "Daddy, can't God do anything?"

In the lives of all of us, there are times when it seems that God doesn't hear, that the earth keeps trembling, that children keep dying, and that God "can't do anything."

The problem of evil is as old as man. Why does a good God, with all power at his disposal, seemingly turn a deaf ear to some of our most heart-searching prayers? We cannot always understand. But we can always trust. We can agree with Abraham who asked, "Shall not the Judge of all the earth do right?" (Gen. 18:25). And with Job who said, "For he will not lay upon man more than [is] right" (34:23) and "Though he slay me, yet will I trust in him" (13:15).

16. Trapped by the past

A pastor of a rather large rural church was showing a visitor through the building. Although the congregation had recently completed a building program, additional space was still needed. When they reached the second floor, the pastor asked the visitor to look out the window on all sides. A large cemetery surrounded the church on three sides—to the left, to the right, and in the back. In the front was the highway.

Half joking, and half serious, the pastor said, "You know, we can't expand any more, for we are surrounded by the dead!"

Surrounded by the dead! Not many churches are closed in on three sides by cemeteries. But some are hemmed in by members who are dead in vision, in progress, and concern. They are dead in that they are concerned only in maintaining the status quo.

Conscientious Christians must never forget that Jesus said that God is "not the God of the dead, but of the living" (Matt. 22:32).

17. Tips for Dads

J. P. Allen, a Baptist minister, once asked a child psychologist, "If you had one rule for fathers, what would it be?" In reply, the psychologist gave him what he called the *ABC's* of discipline.

A, he said, stands for always. "Always be consistent. Maintain a reasonable level of discipline with your child. If you blow your stack because he leaves the cap off the toothpaste today and then say nothing when he damages the neighbor's property tomorrow, you confuse him."

B, he said, stands for busy. "But not too busy. Some of the worst jobs of fatherhood are by men of good reputation who copped out under the guise of 'too busy.' If you're not too busy to have a kid, then don't alibi out of giving him the time and friendship he rightly expects. It's not a matter of being busy, but of being disorganized or not caring. If you allow yourself to be too preoccupied, your youngster will read it as rejection."

C, he said, stands for caring. "Men are equal partners in parenthood. It's not woman's work to rear the young. She may have to supervise them during work hours, but there's evenings, weekends, holidays, and vacations when you can show you care. A major peril to children in America is the bad parenthood of good men."

18. Broken windows

Paul asked a very searching question in 1 Corinthians 3:16, "Know ye not that ye are the temple of God, and that the Spirit of God dwelleth in you?" Then he went on to say in verse 17, "If any man defile the temple of God, him shall God destroy."

We would not think of desecrating and vandalizing a beautiful church building. We would not throw bricks through its stained-glass windows, pour paint on its carpets, or write vulgar and profane words on its walls. Yet in our thoughtlessness we sometimes defile our bodies through poor health habits. And is that not much worse than defacing a church building?

A recent study shows that Seventh-day Adventists (who avoid tobacco, liquor, and coffee) have 40 percent fewer diseased heart arteries than the rest of us. And their blood-cholesterol level is 15 percent lower than the general population. Clean living is not only good religion—it's also good sense.

19. Determined to run

"If you don't let me run, I'll tear the gym apart brick by brick," threatened Jim Borden when he was a student at State University of New York. Borden, who broke the two-mile school record during his senior year in 1969–70, made the threat to the university's physician who didn't want to clear him for varsity sports.

The reason? Jim was born with a disease called ichthyosis (from the Greek, "fish disease"). His body overproduces keratin, which gives the skin a dry, scaly appearance. In severe cases, sweat and oil glands are often missing, meaning the body can't readily disperse excess heat through perspiration.

Because of Jim's inability to sweat, his doctor warned him not to take part in sports. But Jim was so insistent ("I'll tear the gym apart") that his teammates found a way. During a track meet, they simply stationed themselves along the route with buckets of water. When Jim passed, they doused him with cool water. The bucket brigade substituted for the sweat glands, and the cooling effect of the evaporating water enabled him to compete without overheating.

Which means that the will to achieve is the most important ingredient in any success.

20. Individualism

In our quest for group decisions and peer approval, we overlook the unique value of the individual. There is security with the crowd but frequent inferiority as well. A conference is often a mere convocation of people who singly can do nothing and collectively decide that nothing can be done.

As the late Whitney Griswold put it, "Could *Hamlet* have been written by a committee or the *Mona Lisa* painted by a club? Could the New Testament have been composed as a conference report? Creative ideas do not spring from groups. They spring from individuals. The divine spark leaps from the finger of God to the finger of Adam."

21. A tiny spark

A news dispatch from British Columbia tells of a disastrous fire in an Indian village that destroyed twenty-one buildings and left fifty homeless. The odd thing is that the fire was started by the rays of the sun reflected against the wooden side of a house by a fragment of a broken mirror. Doubtless no one even noticed the mirror or was aware when the first little curl of smoke gave initial warning of the coming conflagration.

The Bible compares the tongue to fire, reminding that a careless word tossed here or there can ignite the whole "course of nature." In James 3:6 we read, "And the tongue is a fire, a world of iniquity: so is the tongue . . . it defileth the whole body, and setteth on fire the course of nature." We would not knowingly focus a mirror onto some highly combustible material, nor would we carelessly throw lighted matches into a dry wheat field. But how often have we in a moment of weakness made some remark which helped us none and which brought searing burns of pain to others.

22. Comin' loose!

In Marc Connelly's play, *Green Pastures,* the angel Gabriel is speaking to God about all the frustrating things that are happening. Here is how he phrased it, "Everything nailed down is coming loose!"

Each generation tends to identify change as peculiar to its own. But change has always haunted man, and the person who cannot adapt to change can never adjust to life. One of the few permanent features of life is change itself.

If you want proof of how each generation fears change, go back forty-eight centuries when an Assyrian wrote the following on a clay tablet, recently dug up in Turkey: "Our earth is degenerate; bribery and corruption are common; children no longer obey their parents; every man wants to write his memoirs; and the end of the world is evidently approaching."

Or to the past century, when a writer in the October 10, 1857, issue of *Harper's* Magazine wrote: "It is a gloomy moment in history. Not for many years has there been so much grave and deep apprehension, and never has the future seemed so incalculable as at this time. In France the political cauldron seethes and bubbles with uncertainty; Russia hangs, as usual, like a cloud, dark and silent, upon the horizon; while all the energies, resources, and influences of the British Empire are sorely tried, and are yet to be more sorely tried."

23. Flabby Christians

A friend of mine, Milo B. Arbuckle, likes to hunt and fish in the Rockies. His jeep often takes him off the beaten paths to where the mountain streams are clearest and the game most plentiful. His specialty is trout, including the rainbow, native, German-brown, and cutthroat.

One of his favorite haunts is about 10,000 feet up in the mountains, where the Rio Grande starts its long, winding descent through Colorado, New Mexico, then slices Texas from Mexico, before emptying into the Gulf of Mexico.

"The best trout are up there," Milo boasts. "It is the nature of trout constantly to move upstream. The weaker and diseased fish are swept downstream. Only the strongest eventually reach the top, where the water is clearest and coldest."

Milo can judge a fish that has struggled upstream, for it is firmer and more muscular. He easily spots a hatchery-bred trout, because it is soft and flabby.

I thought of the hymn, "Higher Ground." It is the nature of a growing Christian to swim upstream. He may not always reach his goal, but his direction is onward and upward, while Christians who drift with the current end up soft and flabby.

24. Another drummer

"If a man does not keep pace with his companions, perhaps it is because he hears a different drummer. Let him step to the music which he hears, however measured or far away."—Henry Thoreau

25. Is humor holy?

On the radio program "MasterControl," Kenneth Chafin described how humor is a part of the Christian life. Among other things, he said:

"I feel sorry for people who have no sense of humor. Life is going to be rough for them. And you don't have to be able to tell a joke to have a sense of humor. Some of the happiest people I know are people who enjoy life to its fullest, but they couldn't tell a joke effectively if their lives depended on it.

"I guess I've always had a sense of humor. Most people think I inherited it from my father. As a result, when I began to be aware of the fact that God was calling me to preach, I wondered what I should do with my sense of humor. So much of the preaching I had been exposed to had such a stern and somber note and was so full of judgment.

"I've now come to believe that laughter and humor are gifts from God. They give us release from the unbearable responsibilities of life. They often give us an alternative to crying. They preserve us from pompousness. Laughing people learn more than crying people. And you know, people who can laugh are usually the same ones with the capacity for seriousness. Humor can be healing. As a matter of fact, learning to laugh at ourselves, with our strutting and our pretensions, may be the prelude to repentance. And, there are times when laughter can become a form of worship of the living God."

26. Silence as disgraceful

During the Adolf Hitler regime in Germany, Rabbi Joachim Prinz served the Jewish community in Berlin. Rabbi Prinz said he learned many things: "But the most important thing I learned—under those tragic circumstances—is that bigotry and hatred are not the most urgent problems. The most urgent, the most disgraceful, the most shameful, and the most tragic problem is silence."

Many years before, Edmund Burke echoed the same sentiments when he warned, "All that is necessary for the triumph
of evil is for good men to do nothing."

27. The Bible's drama

Billy Sunday's word picture of the Bible illustrates the heroic
and dramatic oneness of the Scriptures. Although his definition
of the Bible may be an oversimplification, it does add drama to
the story of redemption:

I entered through the portico of Genesis and walked down through the
Old Testament art gallery where the pictures of Abraham, Moses, Joseph,
Isaiah, David, and Solomon hung on the walls.

I passed into the music room of the Psalms and every reed of God's
great organ responded to the tuneful harp of David.

I entered the chamber of Ecclesiastes where the voice of the preacher
was heard, and into the conservatory of Sharon and the lily of the valley's
spices filled and perfumed my life.

I entered the business office of the Proverbs, then into the observation
room of the prophets where I saw telescopes of various sizes, some
pointing to far-off events but all concentrated upon the bright star which
was to rise above the moonlit hills of Judea for our salvation.

I entered the audience room of the King of kings and passed into the
correspondence rooms where sat Matthew, Mark, Luke, John, Peter, Paul,
and James penning their epistles.

I stepped then into the throne room of Revelation and caught a vision
of the King sitting on his throne in all his glory, and I cried:

> "All hail the power of Jesus' name!
> Let angels prostrate fall;
> Bring forth the royal diadem,
> And crown Him Lord of all."

28. The minister's role

When Floyd D. Shafer was pastor of the Salem Presbyterian
Church in Salem, Indiana, he made some pointed suggestions
to ministers. Feeling the average pastor gives too much time to
promotion, he advised:

1. Remove the sign which says "office" and go back to the
use of "study" to designate his place of work.

2. Take him off the promotional mailing list and lock him up with his Bible, all kinds of good books, and his typewriter.

3. Insist that he be the one man in the community who takes time to pray, study, and think. Demand that he give forty hours a week to these pursuits.

4. "Bend his knees in the lonesome valley."

5. Remove him from the PTA, get him out of the country club, take out his telephone, and put water in the gasoline tank of his "community buggy" (car).

While some of us would not be so drastic, there is a general recognition that the pastor should major on his role as a spiritual advisor and leader. This will come when laymen assume more routine tasks and pastors discipline themselves to the rigors of systematic study, prayer, and meditation.

29. Seizing the initiative

When Norris W. Fulfer was a student pastor at Golden State Baptist Theological Seminary in California, he often picked up hitchhikers while driving back from his church field on Sunday evenings.

One night he picked up a sailor headed for Treasure Island, after a weekend leave. The young serviceman sprawled comfortably in the minister's car and told how tired he was after being up all Saturday night. He described how he and his girl friend had done about everything moral and immoral in the books and what a wonderful time he had.

Fulfer listened courteously until the sailor was finished, then said he would like to describe his weekend services and also share what Christ meant to him as a personal Savior and friend.

Very quickly the hitchhiker said that he was too tired to listen and that he was going to take a nap. The minister then stopped his car on the edge of the dark highway and reached across to open his passenger's door. "You have been my guest," Fulfer explained. "I have listened courteously to you. Now if you cannot show me the same courtesy, perhaps you had better walk back to the base."

To say the least, the sailor had a quick change of heart, and immediately straightened up in the seat to listen. As the student preacher shared Christ, the sailor made a profession of faith right there driving along the highway. Fulfer could have been turned off or have taken the sailor's retort as an insult. Instead, with courtesy and tact, he seized the opportunity to make a positive witness for Christ.

30. Facing sorrow

A sign over a welding shop read, "We mend everything except a broken heart and the break of day."

Sorrow and trouble are more bearable when shared with others, but inevitably, each man must bear his own burden, and shed his own tears. As John Donne once said, ". . . never send to know for whom the bell tolls; it tolls for thee."

The cruelest advice is often the injunction, "Don't cry." Better that the tears should flow and that the grief run its normal course, than to be bottled up inside. "He that lacks time to mourn, lacks time to mend." A cloudless day never produced a rainbow. It shares its bright hues only with those who first endure the storm.

31. The fourth astronaut

When an oxygen tank exploded aboard Apollo 13 at 10:08 P.M. on the night of April 13, 1970, the lives of three astronauts hung in the balance for four anxious days. Although its $380 million mission was to place man on the moon for the third time in history, the flight was aborted 207,000 miles out in space.

Worldwide attention was focused on the plight of astronauts James A. Lovell, Jr., Fred W. Haise, Jr., and John L. Swigert, Jr. Special prayers were offered in thousands of churches. Thirteen nations, including the Soviet Union, offered ships or planes if needed in the rescue operation. The U.S. embassy in London said there had been no such outpouring of concern since John Kennedy's assassination.

During the interminable wait, families of the astronauts were inundated with requests for interviews, comments, and reaction. One of the most significant was made by one of the fathers, J. Leonard Swigert, a Denver ophthalmologist. "There's a fourth astronaut," he said, "riding in the capsule with them." In a televised interview, astronaut Swigert was asked if the "infinite played a role in your recovery?" He replied, "If you mean do I believe in prayer, the answer is Yes. I prayed, and I believe God directed us."

32. The world is watching

From the deck of the little 350-ton *Arbella* plowing westward through the angry Atlantic Ocean to the coast of Massachusetts in 1630, John Winthrop preached a mighty sermon that set the pace of what America in all its future would seek to be.

As the United States, the world's richest, strongest nation, approaches its 200th birthday in 1976, Winthrop's words should make us reevaluate our national goals:

Wee shall be as a Citty upon a Hill, the Eies of all people are uppon us: so that if wee shall deale falsely with our god in this worke wee have undertaken and soe cause him to withdrawe his present help from us, wee shall be made a story and a by-word through the world.

33. The influence of love

More than 50 years ago at Johns Hopkins University in Baltimore, a young sociology professor assigned his class to a city slum to interview 200 boys. "On the basis of your findings, predict their future," he said.

Shocked at what they found in the slums, the students estimated that 90 percent of the boys interviewed would someday serve time in prison.

Twenty-five years passed. The same professor asked another class to try to locate the survivors of the 200 boys and compare what had happened. Of 180 of the original boys located, only four had ever been to jail.

Why had the predictions not turned out? A common denominator was sought in their lives, some value or influence that may have marked the difference. Through more interviews, it was found that over 100 of the men remembered having the same high-school teacher, a Miss O'Rourke, who had been a tremendous influence on them at the time. After a long search, Sheila O'Rourke was found in a nursing home in Memphis, now 70 years old. When asked for her explanation, she was puzzled. "All I can say," she concluded, "is that I loved every one of them."

34. Intelligence is Godlike, too

One of the most awesome displays of nature is a total eclipse of the sun, turning noonday into darkness and sending chickens to roost hours before their bedtime.

There was only one total eclipse of any great duration in this century in the United States, and that was on March 7, 1970. The previous one of comparable duration in the United States was in 1878, and the next one isn't due until 2024!

The first recorded eclipse was on October 22, in the year 2137 B.C. It was logged by a couple of Chinese astronomers, Hsi and Ho. (But according to tradition, Hsi and Ho were beheaded by the emperor because they had been drinking the night before and slept through the eclipse. Supposedly, they were to be awake to shoot arrows at an imagined "dragon" who was "eating" the sun!)

The pinpoint precision with which the planets move through the heavens, enabling astronomers to predict their exact location centuries in advance, is one of the greatest evidences of a divine intelligence.

We speak freely of the love, glory, power, and justice of God. Do we magnify his intelligence as we should?

We say that the more one shows love, the more he is like

God. Likewise, we should say that the more intelligent man becomes, the more he is like God. God performs many wonders through dedicated men, in spite of their weaknesses. Can he not do more through the equally dedicated, but highly intelligent individual?

"Lord, I thank you that I'm ignorant, and I just pray you will make me more ignoranter" is always good for a laugh and two of three amens. You may label such gibberish as simple faith, but it's more like an insult to God.

"When I consider thy heavens, the work of thy fingers, the moon and the stars, which thou hast ordained; What is man . . . ?" (Ps. 8:3–4).

35. The lights couldn't go off

When Thomas A. Edison died on October 18, 1931, President Herbert Hoover suggested that all the lights in America be turned off for one minute in honor of the noted inventor. It was when he was only thirty-two that the youthful inventor, after thirteen months of repeated failure, had developed the first incandescent light. It was, in his words, the "most difficult" of all his inventions.

But President Hoover's proposal was never carried out, because responsible leaders decided that too much risk would be involved if all lights were suddenly extinguished at the same time.

Edison designed a product that proved indispensable. Even at his death, the world could not do without it for a single minute. A good test of any man's life is whether he makes even a small contribution which just one person cannot do without.

36. Getting attention

Many Bible stories can be illustrated with common, everyday objects. The purpose is to draw and hold attention. You tap the added value of visual as well as verbal communication. The object will not necessarily convey a "lesson" in and of itself. But the object focuses attention on what you have to say.

Here are a few examples. With a little imagination, you can think of dozens more. Children will readily respond to them. Adults, being more reserved, will also respond but may not admit it!

Let's say you are speaking on the tragedy of Jacob and Esau, those twin brothers who could not get along. Finally, Jacob was forced to leave home. His first night away, sleeping by the roadway, he dreamed of a ladder reaching to heaven. Angels were ascending and descending. Now, why not take a small ladder or stepladder into the pulpit or classroom with you? Use it as a prop to your message. Childish? Crude? Undignified? That depends on how you present it. The ladder itself illustrates nothing. It is merely a visual to capture attention.

Or you are preaching on the Old Testament story of David's fight with Goliath. Why not display a slingshot and five, smooth rocks?

You are teaching the story of the feeding of the five thousand and the generosity of the lad who had shared his two fishes and five loaves? Why not use an ordinary lunch box to catch attention?

When Jesus talked with the woman at a well in the village of Sychar, he impressed her with the need for living, spiritual water. So use an old-fashioned water bucket, with a rope fastened to it. Throw in a little nostalgia for the older folks who remember drawing water from wells. Point out that neither the old-fashioned water bucket nor modern water pumps can supply the spiritual water which forever quenches one's thirst.

If you are speaking on the seven churches of Asia in Revelation 1:12–20, utilize a seven-tiered candelabra. Light each of the candles to symbolize the seven churches, and picture Christ's intimate relationship to his churches. (For additional suggestions see *Devotional Talks on Everyday Objects,* Robert J. Hastings, Nashville: Broadman Press, 1968.)

37. A glass darkly

Shatter-resistant plastic is taking the place of many windows in schools, churches, and business places subject to vandalism. The new plastic windows have the advantage of resisting rocks and other projectiles. But a disadvantage is that images seen through the plastic are slightly distorted.

Life is often distorted and out of focus, and its sharpness is curtailed when we abuse the laws of nature, whether it be a pane in a store window or one of the Commandments. Man can't go around breaking the windows of the universe and still see the glories of the rainbow with the eyes of an angel.

"For now we see through a glass, darkly" is the way Paul expressed it in 1 Corinthians 13:12. Yet our goal is to see life as it is, face to face, unmarred by man's frailties.

38. Make-shift religion

If you are one of those persons who boasts, "I can worship just as well at home," here is some good advice by Hartwell Daley:

Do-It-Yourself Religion, Complete with Home Funeral Service

Why support someone else to do something you can do as well by yourself. Send today for our new Do-It-Yourself Workshop Kit!

Here's what you'll find in each carefully planned package:

One portable, lightweight seat, shaped like a church pew. Can be set up anywhere.

One small, paper-covered hymnal containing one dozen well-known hymns (words and music).

One harmonica—or mouth organ—to take the place of the church organ. (Frankly, you will find it difficult to play and sing at the same time. But you can master it, and after all there must be some challenge.)

One abbreviated New Testament with familiar selections designed to be read in less than one minute each.

One small offering plate—to be held in the left hand while putting coin in with the right. (Denomination of the coin is unimportant as you will get it back anyway.)

One brief sermon entitled "What a Good Boy Am I." You will feel much better after using this sermon. It may be read aloud or silently.

Those who have used our Do-It-Yourself Workshop Kit tell us they get an extra lift from their own service if at the close, they rush to a mirror and shake hands with themselves. But this is optional.

39. A disgrace

When some Christians talk about the "grace of giving," their practice would come nearer being labeled the "disgrace of giving."

40. 'Spoiled' by kindness

In an experiment with rats at Queen's University in Kingston, Ontario, a lab technician showered love and affection on the rodents, even giving them names! When she administered lethal doses of drugs for experimental purposes, only 20 percent died, whereas the same dose given by anyone else killed an average of 80 percent! Even as she started to give the drugs via a painful stomach tube, the rats literally ran to her, offering little or no resistance.

In Plymouth, Michigan, ex-GI and K-9 instructor Charles T. Art runs a school for watchdogs. Here he trains German shepherds who guard industrial plants, sniff out hidden narcotics, and join police departments. He emphasizes that he does not train "killers," but rather dogs who obey their handlers. The ideal recruit? Mr. Art says it is a six-month-old dog brought up with young children, kids who preferably have spoiled the puppy with kindness!

And then Dr. John Gilmore of Boston University says that lack of attention in the home is one of the chief factors that separate low achievers from high achievers. Boys and girls who come from families where the parents show physical affection in the form of hugs and kisses, e.g., tend to make better grades.

Rats in a lab, dogs in Michigan, and kids in school. Is there a correlation in these isolated stories? I think so, and it is found in 1 Corinthians 13:13, ". . . but the greatest of these is love (RSV)." Love still accomplishes more than hate, violence, and punishment. It is a common thread of the universe, touching man and animals alike.

41. For spite, at least

J. B. Gambrell, pioneer Texas Baptist leader, displayed his wit and insight in an article which he called, "Killing Lizards." Here is one of his illustrations:

A farmer sent his son Charlie to the field to lay by a promising crop of corn. About the middle of the afternoon, he walked down to the field to see how the plowing was going on. To his amazement, Charlie was running hither and yon, thrashing and knocking down the corn, as if trying to kill something. About half an acre of corn was already beaten down.

"Charlie, what in the world is the matter?" he hollered out.

"I was just taking a nap, and something like a lizard ran over me, and I'm trying to kill it."

To which his dad replied, "Now see what you've done. Half the afternoon is gone, as well as half an acre of corn. What is the use of killing this lizard, anyway? Is it worth all that?"

"I don't care," Charlie called back. "I'm going to kill him if it takes the whole crop."

42. "Just a Baptist"

A friend of mine, James H. Smith, was returning with his family from the meeting of the Baptist World Alliance in Miami, Florida, the summer of 1965. They stopped to spend the night in Valdosta, Georgia, and after checking in the motel, stepped across the street to a restaurant. The fifteen-year-old daughter of the owner was their waitress. In serving the meal, she accidentally spilled the entire tray of mashed potatoes, roast beef, cole slaw, iced tea, rolls and butter in the middle of the floor.

A busboy came and rather half-heartedly cleaned up the mess.

But the floor was still slippery from water, salad dressing, and mustard when he went for a mop. Just then the waitress returned, this time with coffee for my friend. He warned her of the slick spot. But not in time! She spilled the whole cup of hot coffee down the front of his coat, tie and shirt. This did it. She dissolved in tears and rushed for the sanctuary of the kitchen.

Instead of exploding, my friend left a note of understanding together with $1.00.

The next morning when he stopped for coffee in another restaurant down the highway, another customer asked, "Aren't you the fellow who got soaked with coffee in Valdosta last night?" Then he added, "If I had been you, I would have cussed the daylights out of that girl." Then he asked why my friend had been so tolerant. My friend replied, "You see, we are Christians. And we just try to practice our religion wherever we are."

Whereupon the questioner dropped his head sheepishly. "Well, I'm just a Baptist."

43. Synthetic sympathy

"Madam," he apologized in a broken voice, "I wish to draw your attention to the terrible plight of a poor family in your neighborhood.

"The father is dead. The mother is too ill to work. And the nine children are hungry. Moreover, they are about to be turned out into the cold, cold streets unless the neighbors pay their rent.

At this point the neighbor asked, "And may I ask who you are?"

Dabbing his eyes with a handkerchief to check a fresh flow of tears, the solicitor confessed, "I am the landlord."

Moral: Are we truly interested in the plight of the other fellow or because his plight will eventually affect us?

44. How good men encourage evil

In 1903, *McClure's Magazine* published a series of exposé articles on corruption in American cities, written by Lincoln

Steffens. The next year, the articles were published under the title *The Shame of the Cities,* one of the most influential books of the nineteenth century.

For his research, Steffens studied organized crime, big league politicians, graft, and corruption in such cities as St. Louis, Minneapolis, Philadelphia, Chicago, and Pittsburgh.

One of Steffens' key discoveries was that corruption often existed with the knowledge and even cooperation of the leading citizens. Great numbers of "good" people never bothered even to register as voters. In St. Louis, he found a graft-ridden political machine backed by men of supposedly high integrity, wealth and social standing, as well as church members and Sunday School teachers.

After studying Minneapolis, he concluded, "No reform I ever studied has failed to bring out this phenomenon of virtuous cowardice, the baseness of the decent citizen."

Toward the end of his book he reasoned, "The misgovernment of the American people is misgovernment by the American people . . . the people are corrupt in small ways as their leaders are in big ways." He saw the average person as avoiding self-government, hoping instead for "a legal machine that will turn out good government automatically," but which in truth never would or could.

And when the noted social reformer Jane Addams founded Hull House in Chicago in 1899, she wrote: "The streets are inexpressibly dirty, the number of schools inadequate . . . the street lighting bad, the paving miserable . . . and the stables foul beyond description . . . Many houses have no water supply save the faucet in the backyard, there are no fire escapes, the garbage and ashes are placed in wooden boxes which are fastened to the street pavement."

To her surprise, she found either antagonism or indifference among the responsible people of her day. On the 100th anniversary of her birth, Archibald MacLeish noted: "It was not the crank who said that Jane Addams ought to be hanged to the nearest lamppost: it was a solid citizen who, like other solid citizens, regarded any legislation aimed at the protection of children in factories as an attack on his right, as a citizen of a free country, to do as he pleased. And it was not an irresponsible newspaper which hounded her as a radical: it was a newspaper most of the responsible people of the city read."

English statesman Edmund Burke (1729–1797) said it in sixteen words, "All that is necessary for the triumph of evil is for good men to do nothing."

45. Satan told him

At times, all of us are displeased with the vanity that we see within. It may help if we can occasionally laugh at ourselves.

At the close of a worship service, someone told John Bunyan he had preached well that day.

"The devil already told me that as I was coming down the pulpit steps," he replied.

46. "It melts in transit"

When I was a boy, we hung a four-cornered card in the window each morning during the summer. The numbers 25, 50, 75, and 100 were printed in the corners.

It was our way of telling the iceman how many pounds to bring. If mother had waxed the kitchen floor, she spread newspapers to catch the dripping water, for ice melts in transit. You never have as much when you get there as when you start.

Time, too, melts in transit. It gets away from us. You never have as much left when you get where you are going as when you left. Some people boast about "saving" time. Hogwash! Ask anyone to show you the time he "saved." You can save money, but you can't save time. It slips away. Oh, you can find quicker ways of doing things. You can cut corners, timewise. But you can't hold time back. You can't put it on deepfreeze, or lock it in a vault, or reverse the pages of the calendar.

James 4:14 reminds us that our life is "even a vapour, that

appeareth for a little time, and then vanisheth away." And Psalm 90:6 compares man to the grass which in the morning flourishes, but in the evening is cut down and withered.

And then the insights of Ecclesiastes 3:1–4, "To every thing there is a season, and a time to every purpose under the heaven: A time to be born, and a time to die; a time to plant, and a time to pluck up that which is planted; a time to kill, and a time to heal; a time to break down, and a time to build up; a time to weep, and a time to laugh; a time to mourn, and a time to dance."

Yes, time, like ice, melts in transit. It's your life! Use it or misuse it, but you can't hold on to it. Which is what some mean when they say it is better to wear out than to rust out!

47. "God is here"

Engraved on the doors of some old churches in England are these words:

> Enter this door
> As if the floor
> Within were gold,
> And every wall
> Of jewell all
> Of wealth untold;
> As if a choir
> In robes of fire
> Were singing here.
> Nor shout, nor rush,
> But hush . . .
> For God is here.

48. Couldn't wait

A farmer in central Illinois, whose main crop was corn, was beset with fear near the end of the planting season one spring that his automatic corn planter had cracked all of the seed. If this. were true, his entire crop would be lost, and there was not time to plant a second time.

Although he had experienced other emotional problems earlier, it was the frustration and anxiety over his corn that ultimately caused him to take his own life.

To add irony to his suicide, his seed corn did germinate and grow, and had he waited only a few days, he would have known that the corn planter had not malfunctioned.

We are quick to pass judgment on a farmer who would sacrifice his life for a single season's corn crop. But impatience, snap judgment, and premature conclusions can lead to regrettable action even in the small things of life. As George Herbert said, "Though God take the sun out of heaven, yet we must have patience."

49. A poor man's gift

Many years ago, about 1875, a homeless tramp died in a Chicago poorhouse. In his ragged coat pocket was found the following will. It has become famous as "The Will of Charles Lounsberry" and has been widely reprinted as an example that some of the best joys of life are free:

"I, Charles Lounsberry, being of sound and disposing mind and memory, do hereby make and publish this my last will and testament.

"Item: I give to good fathers and mothers, in trust for their children, all good little words of praise and encouragement, and all quaint pet names and endearments; and I charge said parents to use them justly, but generously, as the deeds of their children shall require.

"Item: I devise to boys jointly, all the useful idle fields and commons where ball may be played, all pleasant waters where one may swim, all snow-clad hills where one may coast, and all streams and ponds where one may fish, or where, when grim winter comes, one may skate, to hold the same for the period of their boyhood.

"Item: To lovers, I devise their imaginary world, with whatever they may need, as the stars of the sky, the red roses by the wall, the bloom of the hawthorn, the sweet strains of music, and aught else they may desire to guarantee to each other the lasting-ness and beauty of their love.

"Item: To young men jointly I bequeath all the boisterous inspiring sports of rivalry, and I give to them the disdain of weakness, and undaunted confidence in their own strength.

"Item: And to those who are no longer children or youths, or lovers, I leave memory; and bequeath to them the volumes of poems of Burns and Shakespeare and other poets, if there be others, to the end that they may live the old days over again, freely and fully without tithe or diminution.

"Item: To the loved ones with snowy crown, I bequeath the happiness of old age, the love and gratitude of their children until they fall asleep."

50. From God

In the middle of the night some years ago, the pastor of the First Baptist Church in Columbus, Ohio, Ray Bailey, was called to a home in one of the poorer sections of the city where a young mother had only a few hours to live.

The six-year-old daughter met him at the door. Looking up into his face, she asked, "Are you from God?"

Ray Bailey started to say, "No, I'm from the First Baptist . . ." but caught himself. Quickly recovering, he said, "Yes, I am from God."

Wherever we take a cup of cold water to the least of God's children, we *are* from God. To some of these in despair, we may be their only visible, tangible link with the divine.

51. A word of encouragement

Most of us can recall from our childhood one or two choice teachers who overshadow the others. One of my favorites was my fifth-grade teacher, Floyd Baggett of Marion, Illinois.

One day he asked each of us to try our hand at writing something original—a little story or a poem. I turned in a "master-piece" about a midnight raider who robbed a pioneer family on the frontier, leaving their cabin in flaming ruins.

In a few days the papers were graded and returned. But when I looked for my grade, I found none. At first I was disappointed. Then I looked at the bottom of the page.

Mr. Baggett had struck the last line, "By Bobby Hastings." Instead he had written, "By Henry W. Longfellow."

Mr. Baggett knew I was not Henry Longfellow, that great nineteenth century American author who immortalized himself with such poems as "Hiawatha" and "The Village Blacksmith."

And I certainly knew I was not Henry Longfellow. But this was Mr. Baggett's way of expressing confidence, of saying a word of encouragement.

I can never forget this little gesture. In my mind's eye, I can still see the flourish of his handwriting, the bold strokes of his pen, and even the color of the ink—medium blue!

"A word fitly spoken is like apples of gold in pictures of silver" (Prov. 25:11).

The poem about the midnight raider is long since gone, but the pat on the back still tingles my spine.

52. Impossible goals

Although not an architect himself, a fellow decided to draw the plans for his new home. Then he employed a builder with the firm understanding that he would follow the blueprints exactly. "You may not like my plans, but they suit me. So don't try to change anything, even if it appears best in your judgment."

The owner was out of town while the house was being framed, but on his return he went immediately to inspect it. With plans in hand, he and the builder checked out the downstairs. "Just like I designed it," he complimented the builder.

"Now let's take a look upstairs," he suggested. But looking around, he was unable to locate the staircase.

"There isn't any," the builder apologized.

The owner was irate. "How could any carpenter in his right mind build a two-story house without a stairway?"

The builder spread out the plans, and recalled the agreement. To his amazement and embarrassment, the owner discovered that he had forgotten to design any steps.

We smile at such naïveté. But all around us are people who want a second story, a third story, or a fourth floor to their lives. They are dissatisfied to live at ground level mediocrity, or to subsist at basement level. Some even have visions of a skyscraper!

But pride and self-confidence rob some of achieving their goals. They brag about being self-made. They need neither God nor anyone else to plan their lives.

That's why some end up with the goal, but no steps to achieve it!

53. It found him

Albert Schweitzer, missionary, musician, biographer, philosopher, and surgeon, turned his back on wealth and prestige when he sailed for Africa in 1913. An old abandoned hen house was his first hospital, an old camp bed his first operating table.

On a trip to the United States, a reporter asked him, "Dr. Schweitzer, have you found happiness in Africa?"

He replied, "I have found a place of service, and that is enough happiness for anyone."

54. Power unlimited

The heavens have many ways of declaring the glory of God (Ps. 19:1). As just one example, measure the radiation energy given off by the sun. If we bought the solar energy given off by the sun in just one 24-hour period, at the rate of ½¢ per kilowatt, and paid for it in silver dollars, do you know how many silver dollars would be required? Plenty! In fact, those dollars would cover the whole earth, ocean and land, one mile deep. But don't stop there. That's just one day's supply of kilowatt power. The sun is expected to give off energy at this rate for the next 30 billion years!

(If this sounds impressive, remember that the sun is only one of some 100 billion stars in our Milky Way galaxy. Some of these starts are 10,000 times brighter than our sun. To grasp the *ABC*'s of God's power, multiply the sun's energy by 100 billion and that by the several trillion galaxies in the universe.)

Peter Stoner, who taught astronomy in American universities for more than 50 years, believes there is a larger percentage of believers among astronomers than any other profession. "An astronomer who is an atheist is mighty hard to find," he says. "You can't study the heavens and see the tremendous order out there without believing in a Designer."

Stoner also says that people make a mistake of trying to localize God. "That's why the Russian cosmonaut who bragged about not seeing God on his little trip made no point at all. You can't find God by looking into space. You see evidence of his *handiwork* there. [But] you only find *him* through faith in his flesh-and-blood revelation, Jesus Christ."

As to heaven, Stoner believes in life after death and that as a Christian believer he will be with Christ. "But I don't place heaven geographically or astronomically," he explains. "I don't visualize heaven as being in some distant solar system or galaxy. Because God is a spirit, certain definite space is not needed."

55. The taste test

How does one understand sugar? I suppose he could do tremendous research on the subject and become quite an authority. He could write volumes on the history of sugar, where and how it is grown, how it is refined, the various sugar products, the number of people employed in sugar-related industries, the tonnage produced, its economic value, and on and on.

Or, one could go into the laboratory and study its chemical makeup, becoming fluent in "sweet" scientific terminology and formulas.

But tasting a single grain of sugar will do more to explain what sugar really is and what it does than all the textbooks ever written or laboratory experiments ever performed.

The same with the Christian faith. We can theorize, analyze, speculate, investigate, question, discuss, and research the subject. But while there is value in this, there is no substitute for personal experience.

This is what Christ meant when he said, "If any man will do his will, he shall know of the doctrine, whether it be of God, or whether I speak of myself" (John 7:17). And the psalmist, when he wrote, "Oh taste and see that the Lord is good: blessed is the man that trusteth in him" (34:8).

56. "Christ, as a light . . ."

The following prayer is part of a nine-stanza hymn often referred to as the "Breastplate of Saint Patrick." Tradition ascribes the hymn to Patrick, who was born in 385 and is credited with the first missionary thrust into Ireland. It is a poem of penetrating beauty.

> CHRIST
> as a light,
> illumine and guide me!
> Christ, as a shield,
> o'ershadow and cover me!
> Christ, be under me!
> Christ, be over me!
> Christ, be beside me,
> on left hand and right!
> Christ, this day be within
> and without me!
> Christ, the lowly and meek,
> Christ, the all powerful,
> Be in the heart of each
> to whom I speak,
> In the mouth of each
> who speaks to me,
> In all who draw near me,
> or see me, or hear me.

57. Tears can heal

If your best friend received good news and immediately broke out in an ear-to-ear grin, you would hardly say to him, "Now Fred, bear up. Get hold of yourself. Act like a man. Control your emotions. Stop laughing. Eventually, you will recover from the shock of this good news."

Yet isn't that exactly what we say when a friend faces the opposite emotion of sorrow? "Now Fred, bear up. Get hold of yourself. Don't cry. Control your emotions. Everything's going to be all right."

Yet it is just as normal to cry when one is sad, as to laugh when one is happy. And we do a disservice to a friend or loved one when we encourage him to bottle up his sorrow. Tears are the gift of God that help to dissolve the bitterness of our grief. And if a person is not permitted to cry normally when he is grief-stricken, his sorrow may break out in some abnormal way months or years to come.

That is why Jesus said, "Blessed are they that mourn: for they shall be comforted" (Matt. 5:4). There is no comfort for those who hide their sorrow. Only those who express grief can find relief from their grief. Ignore sorrow and it stays around forever. Embrace it, and eventually it leaves. Tears irrigate the soil of human sorrow. Tears turn troubles into trellises along which the vines of faith climb to the sunshine of God's healing power.

At the grave of Lazarus, "Jesus wept" (John 11:35). In this gesture, he showed his humanity. He demonstrated that even the divine Son of God is touched by sorrow. By his example, he taught that it is all right for us to weep, also. Only those who are unafraid to weep over losses have courage to rebuild their broken dreams.

58. Plenty of seeds

Judge Frank Ryburn of Dallas tells about the death of a prominent and benevolent citizen of his city. Judge Ryburn said that after the funeral service he stood outside the home beside an aged Negro servant. It took three trucks to carry the flowers his friends had sent. As they watched the wreaths being loaded for transfer to the cemetery, the judge remarked, "Mr. A surely has lots of flowers, doesn't he?"

The old Negro thought for a minute, then answered. "Yassuh. But you know, he been planting the seeds for them flowers a long time."

59. Not the building

On a visit to England in 1965, I worshiped in two cathedrals— York and Coventry. It was a study in contrasts, one very formal and the other rather folksy.

At York, the day was cloudy, cool, rainy and dark. Only a few tourists wandered around the vast labyrinths of this awe-inspiring church which was started in 1277 and took 230 years to build. It being late afternoon, I stayed for the Evensong. A mere dozen of us felt swallowed up in this vast edifice that would hold thousands. We sat in the richly ornamented, handcarved choir stalls. From the far end of the cathedral, the soft voices of a boy's choir echoed against the thick, stone walls. Hauntingly beautiful, the music grew louder as the procession neared. For about twenty minutes the liturgical service progressed with Scripture reading, prayers, response, and a number by Bach. And again the voices of the boy's choir dying in the recessional.

A few days later I was at Coventry, where a new and modern cathedral stands beside the blackened ruins of the old one, destroyed in an eight-hour bombing raid one November night in 1940. A part of the old altar still stands on which rests a wooden cross shaped from two blackened timbers that fell from the burning roof. And behind the cross the inscription, "Father, forgive them." In contrast with York, it was a bright, sunny day, and hundreds of tourists were there. Then I stepped inside the Chapel of Unity, a small, circular room simply furnished, A large, plain cross hung from the ceiling. An Anglican priest rose to begin the service. And would you believe it? Looking around at the group he announced, "Can anyone here play the piano?" The informality with which he asked for a volunteer and with which he conducted the service, made me feel as if I were in a little country church in Kentucky.

When is one truly worshiping—in a well-ordered service, precise and punctual? Or in an informal one where the leader asks for someone to play the piano and volunteers to fill the choir?

Well, you can't judge it on that basis. Neither formality nor informality is a criteria of worship. The key is sincerity, as Jesus said to the Samaritan woman at Jacob's well, "the true worshippers shall worship the Father in spirit and in truth" (John 4:23).

60. Who is good?

In his commentary on Matthew, William Barclay says, "A man's life must not only be sterilized from evil; it must be fructified to good."

Virtue is not a vacuum. Man is good not merely by refraining from evil, but by embracing what is good.

Who is a wealthy man? One with no debt? Hardly. He could be debt free, yet penniless. Wealth is accumulated capital.

Who is a healthy person? One with no illness, no contagious disease, no infections? Not necessarily. Healthiness includes an abundance of physical and mental strength, not just the absence of disease.

Who is an educated person? One who has an open mind, with no prejudices, no superstitutions? Not necessarily so. His mind could be empty as well as open.

Who is popular? A person with no enemies? Not necessarily. You could have no enemies, and still have no friends.

Likewise, a good man is not necessarily a man without sin. Virtue is something you *do*. As one lady testified, "The Lord saved me from a rocking chair."

61. Is temptation a sin?

When does temptation become a sin? Where is the line that separates the deed from the desire?

A four-year-old girl whom we shall call Betty is riding her tricycle in the backyard, when out of the corner of her eye she sees her mother come outside with a wastebasket. Betty watches as her mother empties the basket, strikes a match to the papers, and returns inside.

At first, Betty pays only casual attention. But in a matter of minutes, she leaves her tricycle to stand by the fire. Then she wonders what might happen if she adds leaves and twigs and trash to the fire.

Soon she is scampering around the yard, picking up anything that will burn. The flames leap higher.

Next, Betty imagines what might happen if she poked the fire, which she immediately proceeds to do. My, how the sparks fly, higher and higher!

She is caught up in a frenzy of making the bonfire bigger and bigger. Suddenly, a spark ignites her dress, and she runs screaming toward her mother, a burning torch. Fortunately, Betty's mother throws her to the ground and wraps her in a rug, squelching the flames and saving her life.

For the sake of speculation, when did Betty's dress catch fire? Had you stood there with a stopwatch, you could have determined the fraction of a second. But potentially, her dress was on fire when she left her tricycle and started toward the fire.

Temptation evolves into sin when desire is translated into action, when we move toward the object of our desire, waiting only for the proper moment.

"If I regard [tolerate, excuse] iniquity in my heart, the Lord will not hear me" (Ps. 66:18). "For as he thinketh in his heart, so is he" (Prov. 23:7).

62. Where freedom ends

A family in Tennessee has handed down a significant letter for at least three generations. William Walter Warmath, a Baptist minister, received it from his mother on his twenty-first birthday, which came while he was serving as a staff member at Ridgecrest Baptist Assembly in North Carolina. He tells about it in his book *Spirit in Conflict*. It had first been written to William's father, J. G. Warmath, on his twenty-first birthday, by his father. Since then, William Warmath has passed it along to his own son, Jerry, on his twenty-first birthday. Here is how the torn pages, yellow with age, read:

Humboldt, Tennessee,
March 24, 1893.

J. G. Warmath, Twenty-one years old today. Free to do as he pleases—to make a first class gentleman, second or third class as you may. Free to associate with first, second or third class ladies and gentleman. Free to be an honor to his family and society generally or otherwise. Free to lead an honorable and upright life, a life that will be esteemed by all who may associate with you. Free to choose your own occupation and make a success or otherwise. Free to love any nice pretty first class young lady and wed her if she is willing. Free to make all the money that you can honorably and save a good living out of it for old age or misfortune. Free to be your own guardian and counsellor—to use all means that may come into your hands as seemeth best to you. But not free to bring reproach upon your Father and Mother's name. . . . Hoping that life may be an honor to your name and country. We subscribe our names—Your Father and Mother.

63. No ear—no tongue

On June 1, 1950, Senator Margaret Chase Smith gave a speech on the floor of the United States Senate deploring the character assassination and hate that was typical of the McCarthy era. Although Senator Joseph R. McCarthy sat behind her as she spoke, she did not mention his name, although she decried the climate of the 50's in which the conservative elements had frightened the liberals into silence, lest they be labeled communistic.

Exactly twenty years later, on June 1, 1970, Senator Smith spoke again on the floor of the United States Senate, this time pointing out that the liberal elements in the country were now so outspoken that they gave no room for the conservatives.

Growing dissatisfaction over the Vietnam War and the presence of National Guardsmen on some college campuses had made the spring of 1970 one of national unrest and turmoil. The Far Left had become increasingly vocal, using obscenities and profanities to drown out any spokesmen for the conservatives. Hard-hat right would not listen to student left, and student left would not listen to hard-hat right.

Senator Smith pointed out that either extreme is bad, whether it be the Communist witch-hunting McCarthy era of the 50's or the New Left of the 70's. She said that an overwhelming majority of Americans believe that:

> Trespass is trespass—whether on the campus or off.
> Violence is violence—whether on the campus or off.
> Arson is arson—whether on the campus or off.
> Killing is killing—whether on the campus or off.

She warned extremists on both sides, and at all levels, that patience ends at the border of violence. Unless an individual can listen to the other person, he has no right to speak for himself, any more than a motorist has a right to use a highway unless he obeys the stop signs.

There is an apparent contradiction in the story of Paul's conversion in Acts 9:7 ("hearing the voice but seeing no one" RSV) and Acts 22:9 ("did not hear the voice of the one who was speaking" RSV). But in 9:7 the genitive case follows the word "hearing," whereas in 22:9 the accusative case follows the word "hearing." The accusative case usually carries the idea of understanding, whereas the genitive may reflect only the awareness of the sound. So those in Paul's party heard a *sound,* but did not understand the *meaning.* Seen thus, there is no contradiction in the two passages.

Here is an important principle for families, neighborhoods, churches, denominations, political parties, and nations. Freedom of speech exists only where all parties are willing to listen to one another. And "listening" means a sincere desire to understand what the other fellow is trying to say. In short, a man who doesn't use his ears should be denied the use of his tongue.

64. Friendship

Frank Crane said that a friend is a person with whom you dare to be yourself. Friendship suggests warmth and companionship. In fact, Dr. Wilfred Funk, noted lexicographer and dictionary publisher, picked what he thought to be the ten most expressive words in the English language. One of the ten is "friendship," which Dr. Funk labels "the warmest word in the English language.

Here are his other nine selections:

> Alone—the bitterest word
> Mother—the most revered
> Death—the most tragic
> Faith—the most inspiring
> Forgotten—the saddest
> Love—the most beautiful
> Revenge—the cruelest
> No—the coldest
> Tranquility—the most peaceful

65. Flame-out

In February, 1970, the burned corpse of twenty-one-year-old Andy Anderson was found in a gasoline-soaked car, a day after he dropped out of the University of Florida. He left a note, describing his losing battle with drugs. After reading it, a coroner's jury in Gainesville, Florida, ruled his death a suicide. Here is Andy's note, reported by *National Observer:*

> The kid flames out.
> I can't seem to fight my battles.
> My mind is no longer my friend.
> It won't leave me alone.
> Please try to understand and forgive.
> Momma and Poppa.
> Why I have done what I have done. I made a terrible mistake with the drug and everyone I have been involved with must pay in hurt and disappointment.
> This Christmas I had a very bad experience with a drug called mescaline.

I have smoked a little pot before—as have many my age—but I tried mescaline only once.

Since then I have not been in control of my mind. I have killed myself because I can no longer run my own affairs, and I can only cause trouble and worry to those who love and care for me.

I have tried to straighten myself out, but things are only getting worse.

Please forgive me, parents, for quitting after you raised me, but I cannot live with myself any longer. What I am trying to say is that my downfall is entirely my own and no one else should ruin their lives because I have ruined mine.

The drug experience has filled me with fear and doubts of myself. I cannot go on. Please try to remember my good points and excuse this final act of desperation.

Mother and father, save yours [lives] by getting involved with something, perhaps helping young people, you are both teachers, from making this same mistake I did.

You were good parents and I love you both, don't let my downfall be yours—you have nothing to be ashamed of. I made the mistake—not you. To those of my friends who might also think about learning about themselves with mind expanding drugs—don't.

Learn about yourself as you live your life—don't try to know everything at once by swallowing a pill. It could blow out all the circuits as it did with me.

I have thought about suicide several times in the past month. I have ruled it out at the last moment knowing how you, my family, would be affected. But I could be nothing but a burden because I can no longer run my life.

There is nothing but misery for all of us should I allow myself to deteriorate further.

I am too weak to fight—too proud to live forever on sympathy of others. Love, Andy.

P.S. A last thought. Don't try to hide my suicide. You can't hide from the world because of this. You did your best but your son made a fatil [sic] mistake.

66. Facing reality

A doctor was surprised to see his patient dressed and ready to go home when he entered his hospital room. At heart, the doctor was glad, for he knew this patient had merely retreated to the security of a hospital bed out of self-pity. "Man, what's happened to you?" the doctor asked with a smile. The patient replied,

"Doctor, I decided it was time for me to get out of this bed and shake hands with reality."

Then there was the fellow who got up each morning just long enough to read the obituary column, and if his name wasn't there, went back to bed!

A mother in a mental institution could not accept the fact that her son, Eddy, was dead. Each day she wrote a letter to Eddy. Each day she addressed an envelope to Eddy. Each day she stamped and mailed it.

One of the surest signs of emotional maturity is the willingness to accept reality, which is another way of saying we accept responsibility for our own actions.

Some people die years before they are buried. The funeral is postponed until rigor mortis sets in. But for all practical purposes, an individual is already dead when he ignores reality, when he insists on writing letters to an Eddy that neither lives nor reads what he writes.

"I have learned, in whatsoever state I am, therewith to be content. I know both how to be abased, and I know how to abound" (Phil. 4:11–12).

67. A psalm of despair

A police officer found the following typewritten note in a telephone booth:

King Heroin is my shepherd, I shall always want. He maketh me to lie down in gutters. He leadeth me beside the troubled waters. He destroyeth my soul. He leadeth me in the paths of wickedness for the effort's sake. Yea, I shall walk through the valley of poverty and will fear all evil for thou, Heroin art with me. The needle and capsule try to comfort me. Thou strippest the table of groceries in the presence of my family. Thou robbest my head of reason. My cup of sorrow runneth over. Surely heroin addiction shall stalk me all the days of my life and I will dwell in the House of the Damned forever.

On the back side, the young woman had written the following:

Truly this is my psalm. I am a young woman, 20 years of age, and for the past year and one half I have been wandering down the nightmare of the junkie. I want to quit taking dope and I try but I can't. Jail didn't cure me. Nor did hospitalization help me for long. The doctor told my family it would have been better, and indeed kinder, if the person who first got me hooked on dope had taken a gun and blown my brains out. And I wish to God she had. My God how I do wish it.

The only thing admirable about her pathetic note is that she admitted her problem was real. And as Norman Vincent Peale says, "Honesty is the beginning of the solution of any problem."

68. What's a book?

I remember vividly the first day of English literature when I was in the eighth grade. Our teacher, Winifred Perry, walked to the chalkboard and wrote, "What is a book?" Then she said, "Bring me your definitions tomorrow."

To ourselves, at least, we snickered. "Doesn't this woman even know what a book is?"

But the next day we discovered she was serious, as each of us took turns reading our definitions. Then she quoted John Milton's classic definition, which I shall never forget: "A good book is the precious lifeblood of a master spirit, embalmed and treasured up on purpose to a Life beyond Life."

In the years since, I have often applied this to the Bible, that Book of books, which truly is the spirit of God himself preserved with paper and ink.

This does not mean the Bible is to be venerated, but rather, it is the teachings of the Bible that have meaning for our lives. A pastor visiting a sick lady, asked if she had a Bible handy, from which he could read to her. "Oh yes," she responded, reaching under her pillow, "I keep one here for good luck all the time!"

During the Vietnam War, a newsphoto showed a soldier holding his bullet-riddled helmet. Inside was a Bible his mother gave him before he left for overseas, and it had helped deflect the bullet. A few days later, another news story described a soldier whose life had been saved by letters from his girl friend, which he, too, had stuffed in the liner of his helmet.

In honesty, was it the Bible as a good luck charm that deflected the bullet, or simply the fact that it was made up of so much protective paper, much like the letters from the girl friend?

We cheapen the Bible to use it like a rabbit's foot. Only when its precious lifeblood becomes our guide and rule does it have any real meaning. Bibles are to be studied, not venerated.

69. Where is God?

A small lad returning from Sunday School was asked by an older gentleman, "Sonny, I'll give you a dime if you'll show me where God is."

The surprising answer, "Mister, I'll give you a dollar if you'll show me where God ain't!"

70. Which ism is worst?

What is the chief enemy of Christianity? Is it humanism, materialism, pantheism, communism, agnosticism, or atheism?

Perhaps the greatest threat to Christianity is none of these, but rather syncretism. What is syncretism? The best synonym is "sincerity." Syncretism says there is good in all religions, and that we should simply cull the best from each. Thus, a sincere seeker will eventually come up with the best from all faiths, or non-faiths.

Syncretism is an ancient ism, and has always been willing to welcome any new religion into its fold. For example, the Babylonians would gladly have added Israel's Jehovah to their long list of gods had not the Jews insisted he was the only God. Likewise, the Romans would have added the Jesus cult to their god-systems. Emperor Alexander Severus, e.g., placed a statute of Christ alongside other deities in his private chapel.

Syncretism is most often expressed in the proverbial saying, "There's good in all religions." While it may be true that most religions have elements of good, this does not necessarily mean that a conglomeration of virtues from each will result in a viable faith.

The New Testament points to Christ as the only hope of salvation, the only avenue to the Father. Acts 4:12 clearly teaches that "there is none other name under heaven given among men, whereby we must be saved." And Matthew 11:27b claims that "neither knoweth any man the Father, save the Son, and he to whomsoever the son will reveal him."

71. The turning point

Many years ago a new teacher was assigned to a one-room school in Indiana. As was customary, the school bullies tried to bluff him the first day. The ringleader drew a comic picture of the new teacher, wrote a few lines under it, and created quite a stir by passing it around the class. Seeing it, the teacher said, "Jim will you please stay after school a few minutes. I want to talk to you."

Jim's friends hung around outside to see what happened. Could the new teacher lick the bully? To their surprise, Jim soon emerged with a book under his arm and went whistling on his way.

The new teacher had disarmed him by saying, "Jim, you have a rare talent. Your ability to write and draw should be developed. I have a book of stories and poems. Would you like to take it home and draw me some pictures to illustrate the stories?"

Thus he fanned to life a spark of latent genius within the overgrown bully, resulting in the turning point of the beloved Hoosier poet, James Whitcomb Riley.

72. A daring ad

In his book *The Hundred Greatest Advertisements,* Julian Watkins reprints one of the most effective ads ever written: "Men wanted for Hazardous Journey. Small wages, bitter cold, long months of complete darkness, constant danger, safe return doubtful."

The ad was written by Sir Ernest Shackleton, explorer of the South Pole, and it ran in London newspapers at the turn of the twentieth century. Regarding response, Shackleton said, "It seemed as though all the men in Great Britain were determined to accompany us."

73. False pride

Although one should not be shattered with an awareness of his weaknesses, it is false pride to pretend we are not human. Only as we admit our limitations can we develop our strengths.

A blind beggar in New York City accepted, rather than denied his problems, when he lettered a crude sign, "My days are darker than your nights."

And when a young fellow applied for a job, furnishing references from his minister and Sunday School teacher, his prospective employer said, "These are good, but we'd like a letter from someone who knows you on weekdays, too."

A pastor, grief-stricken and bitter over the sudden loss of a child, threw himself into his work, preaching even more forcefully than ever. But all of this was a false front for the hidden sores of grief. Then he reached a time of self-understanding, of self-acceptance. Lowering his bluff, he used some of his messages to confess his unresolved doubts and bitterness. Whereupon his congregation took new interest in his sermons. "Why, he has problems and doubts just like the rest of us," they said.

74. Feeling needed

Everyone likes to feel that he is needed.

A rancher's wife was rushed to the hospital with a ruptured appendix. Despite a successful operation and numerous transfusions, she grew steadily worse. The doctor challenged her, "I thought you would try to be strong like John, your husband."

"But John is so strong, he doesn't need me," she confessed. And it was true that John was a strong, self-sufficient individual who seldom expressed his feelings.

That night the doctor told John he didn't think his wife wanted to live. But they would try one more transfusion, direct from John to his wife's veins. As he lay beside her for the transfusion he said, "I'm going to make you well."

"Why?" she asked.

"Because I need you," John answered.

Turning her head slowly she said, "You never told me that before."

She lived. Later the doctor wrote, "It wasn't the transfusion but what went with it."

75. Not there

A placard on a city bus in Minneapolis read, "In this day every American needs to find God—Go to church Sunday." But some wag had written in pencil at the bottom, "I went and he was not there."

76. The ABC's of genius

One mark of a genius may be his ceaseless quest for something better, a holy dissatisfaction with anything short of perfection.

Such must have been the spirit of Michelangelo, 1475–1564, the most famous artist of the Italian Renaissance. He successfully combined four professions, being an artist, sculptor, poet, and architect.

Michelangelo is remembered for such masterpieces as his *Pieta,* now in St. Peter's in Rome, *David,* in the Florence Academy, the Sistine Chapel whose 5,595 square-foot ceiling is painted with his immortal frescoes, and the design of St. Peter's Church, the dome of which has become the standard for similar edifices the world over.

Michelangelo was thirty-four when he started on the Sistine Chapel frescoes, which took four and one-half years of labor, working day and night. To paint the ceilings, he lay on his back on scaffolds sixty to seventy feet high.

First, he gave that portion of the ceiling to be painted that day a fresh coat of plaster. While it was wet, he traced drawings on it. Then he applied liquid paint. As the plaster dried, a chemical reaction bound wall and painting solidly together. Since the paint had to be applied while the plaster was damp, swift, sure strokes were necessary. Paint dripped into his beard, soaking it. Some nights he fell exhausted into bed, not even troubling to undress.

Now crouching, now kneeling, and now lying prone, he strained "like a Syrian bow," forgetting food and sleep, not changing his clothes for months. (When he removed his stockings, his skin peeled off with them.)

When finished, the masterpiece included 434 figures, some twelve feet tall, a stupendous visualization of the biblical account of creation, of man, and of evil.

Yet when this eighty-nine-year-old genius neared death, he said, "I regret . . . that I am dying just as I am beginning to learn the alphabet of my profession."

77. Worship anywhere?

"But I don't have to be in church to worship. I can worship God at home, or driving down the highway, or playing on the golf course."

Perhaps. But listen to what a little girl said to her father. He was taking the family on a Sunday outing and had said they could pray at the lake:

"We could Daddy, but we won't, will we?"

78. Excuses, excuses

Ever since Jesus described the man who made a great supper, only to find that one of his guests could not come because he was recently married, another because he had to prove five yoke of oxen, and another who had just purchased a piece of ground, men have apologized as to why they could not follow the Lord (Luke 14:15–20). And if one is looking for excuses, one is as good as another.

In the early days of the space program, astronauts in training at Cape Kennedy got all kinds of fan mail, much of it from kids. Frequently these youngsters asked to make space trips—but usually with reservations. Some typical letters:

"I am interested in space and would like to become an astronaut, but it will have to be on a Saturday as I go to school during the week."

"I would like to go to the moon with you. I am not afraid, but if possible I would like to come back, too."

"I would like to be a space pilot, but I don't think I can pass the physical because I have fillings in my teeth."

"I have always wanted to be an astronaut, but thought I couldn't because of my nearsightedness. But now I understand space pilots can wear contact lenses. So as soon as I save up enough money to buy some, I would like to be an astronaut, particularly since I know you will need younger men. I am only 10."

79. "Are you happy?"

My ministry has been divided between the pastorate and denominational service. I was a pastor first, then entered the denomination. Later I switched back to the pastorate, and still again to a denominational post.

Persons in church-related vocations are often asked, "Are you happy in your work?" I suppose this is true of all vocations, but it seems to be a rather stock-in-trade query among the religious vocationists. And a rather stock, if sometimes hypocritical, answer is, "Yes, never been happier in my life. I'm just where the Lord wants me to be."

Although I have had a rather constant assurance of serving in God's will, I have shied away from such stock answers. After one of my shifts in employment, here is how I answered a friend:

"Yes, I'm happy because I want to be happy, and not because of where I am or am not. Places and circumstances never guarantee happiness. You must decide within yourself whether you want to be happy. And once you've decided, happiness comes much easier."

I continued, "Happiness is elusive. Never think you can corner it where it can't get away from you. Happiness slips up on you. Happiness overwhelms you. Happiness is a by-product of losing yourself in something you believe to be worthwhile. Happiness comes to those who *act* happy, not those who are desperately seeking. If you look for happiness too hard, the dust you stir up in the effort blinds you to its reality."

80. Maybe why

When Ellis A. Fuller was president of Southern Baptist Theological Seminary in Louisville, Kentucky, he was criticized for raising money for the construction of the Alumni Chapel, instead of putting up dormitories for families.

One critic told him, "And if I were president, I wouldn't waste all that money on a steeple."

To which Fuller replied, "Maybe that's why the Lord didn't let you be president!"

81. Love is unafraid

Soon after his marriage, the famous nineteenth century Irish poet and composer Thomas Moore was called away on business. On his return, he was met not by his beautiful bride, but their family doctor. "Your wife is upstairs. But she has asked you not to come up. She has smallpox. The disease has left her once flawless skin pocked and scarred. She has drawn the shutters, and asked that you never see her again."

Thomas Moore would not listen, but bounded up the steps to his wife's room. It was black as night inside. He reached for the gas jets. "No! Don't light the lamps," screamed his bride. "Go. Please go. This is the greatest gift I can give you, now."

Instead of leaving, he spent most of the night writing a love poem, which he then set to music. The next morning, in her darkened bedroom, he sang:

> Believe me, if all those endearing young charms,
> Which I gaze on so fondly today,
> Were to change by tomorrow, and flee in my arms,
> Like fairy gifts fading away,

Thou wouldst still be adored, as this moment thou art . . .
Let thy loveliness fade as it will,
And around the dear ruin each wish of my heart
Would entwine itself verdantly still . . .

The song ended. His bride rose to her feet, crossed the room, and slowly drew open the shutters. Love was unafraid of the light of reality.

82. Over-selling

Whether one is preaching a sermon or selling vacuum cleaners, it is possible to talk one's self out of a sale by long-windedness.

Such as the visitor who decided he would make a $5.00 contribution. But it was one of those churches where the custom is to receive the offering after the sermon. When the first twenty-five minutes of the sermon was completed, the visitor had cut his intended offering back to $1.00. The preacher droned on and on, repeating himself and murdering the sermon with slow strangulation. After forty-five minutes, the visitor had cut his offering to fifty cents. And after an hour, to a dime. By the time the offering was received, he had decided to take $5.00 *out* of the plate!

83. Some "accident"

Some say that creation was the result of chance. Others say it was God.

Those who rely on chance have some big explaining to do. Here is one simple illustration of the improbability of man just "happening."

Take ten pennies and mark them 1 to 10. Put them in your pocket and give them a good shake. Now try to draw them out of your pocket in order, from 1 to 10, returning each coin to your pocket after each try.

Your chance of drawing number 1 on the first try is 1 in 10. Your chance of drawing 1 and 2 in succession would be 1 in 100. On drawing 1, 2, and 3 in succession, one in a thousand. Your chance of drawing 1, 2, 3, and 4 in succession would be one in 10,000, and so on.

Now listen to this. Your chance of drawing the pennies in perfect succession, 1 to 10, would be one chance in ten billion!

And yet there are some who say that all the complex and essential conditions for life on our earth as we know it could have occurred in the proper sequence just by "chance."

Leslie Weatherhead said, "It demands more of credulity to imagine that the universe was all a huge accident than to believe in the operation of a mind. How very strange that a ball of matter accidentally happening, and accidentally moving round the sun, should accidentally and purposelessly produce a man who purposefully seeks truth and purposefully asks how such an accident could happen, thus exhibiting a more profound degree of intelligence than that which accidentally produced this amazing universe."

84. Up and down

A large company was reclassifying its employees and sent each a questionnaire. The goal was to determine the exact duty of each worker, as compared with his understanding of his responsibilities. The elevator operator had unusual trouble with the question, "How much time do you spend at each of your task assignments?"

After much pondering he wrote, "Up, 50 percent. Down, 50 percent."

Which reminds us of the spiritual, "Sometimes I'm up, sometimes I'm down, O, yes, Lord . . ."

85. The power of hunger

Jesus taught that those who hunger for righteousness will be filled (Matt. 5:6). When a person is desperately hungry for physical food, he becomes oblivious to all else in his search for it. Likewise, when one is sufficiently hungry for spiritual food, he forgets everything in his struggle for it.

As an example of how indifferent a hungry person can be,

Viktor E. Frankl describes the three years he spent in the German slave labor camps at Auschwitz and Dachau during World War II. In his book *Man's Search for Meaning,* he says, "When the last layers of subcutaneous fat had vanished, and we looked like skeletons disguised with skin and rags, we could watch our bodies beginning to devour ourselves . . ."

He illustrates how his own hunger made him indifferent to the sufferings of others. One cold, dark winter morning they were awakened as usual with three shrill blows of a whistle. They tussled with their wet shoes, into which they could scarcely force their feet, sore and swollen with edema. On this particular morning, he heard a prisoner, ordinarily brave and dignified, cry like a baby because his shoes were too shrunken to wear, and he had to go to the snowy marching grounds in his bare feet. Dr. Frankl said, "In those ghastly minutes, I found a little bit of comfort, a small piece of bread which I drew out of my pocket and munched with absorbed delight."

Another day, lying in a hut for typhus patients, Frankl watched with unconcern the death of a fellow patient. Other prisoners grabbed his last, uneaten, messy meal of potatoes, his wooden shoes, his coat, and yes, even a piece of string! They dragged the body outside, the head of the corpse bumping down the steps. "While my cold hands clasped a bowl of hot soup from which I sipped greedily," Frankl recalls, "I happened to look out the window. The corpse which had just been removed stared in at me with glazed eyes. Two hours before, I had spoken to that man. Now I continued sipping my soup."

If a Christian can be as hungry for righteousness as a starving man is for bread, what force can possibly keep him from being filled? Which is another way of saying that we are as good as we want to be!

86. "I'll do it!"

Sometimes we waste both God's time and our own when we pray for him to do what we can do ourselves.

In a midweek service, a prayer request was made for a poor widow in need of fuel and food.

Finally a deacon rose to pray, mentioning most of the objects requested. He closed by saying, "And as far as the widow is concerned, I am able to take care of her needs and will do so tonight after prayer meeting."

87. A job or a calling?

Proverbs 22:13 is a picturesque description of a fellow who gets up some morning and doesn't want to go to work. Here's how it reads, "The slothful man saith, There is a lion without, I shall be slain in the streets." His wife peeks out the window, but sees no lion. His children peer fearfully through the curtains, but see no lion. But to him, the lion is real, at least in his imagination, for he wants to stay home that day.

An occasional reluctance to go to work is normal. But when an individual sees lions on his doorstep each morning, something is more at fault than his eyesight!

His problem may be that he has a job, but not a calling. Max Lerner says a mere job has three characteristics: we want to get it over with the least possible effort, we want to finish it in the shortest possible time, and we want as much pay as possible. On the other hand, a calling is something you could no more help doing than you could help breathing.

This was Robert Louis Stevenson's philosophy, "If a man love the labor of his trade apart from any question of success or fame, the gods have called him."

Winston Churchill said there are two kinds of people. First, those whose work is work and pleasure is pleasure. And second, those whose work and pleasure are one. For the latter, he says, their working hours are never long enough. Each day is a holiday. And when ordinary holidays come, they are grudged as enforced interruptions in an absorbing vocation.

88. How rich?

The December 3, 1965, issue of *Time* told how six young Americans, all under forty, had become millionaires. The six were described as brilliant, somewhat egotistical, and with an insatiable desire to succeed. *Time* said they worked long, hard hours and had little time for their families or recreation. One of the six, Arthur Carlsberg, a real-estate developer in Los Angeles, was reported to be so busy he rarely saw his three sons. The article did mention that Carlsberg took off one week a year to spend with his boys, plus their birthdays.

A week later, this letter to the editor appeared in the December 10 issue:

"Arthur Carlsberg, you report, is a millionaire. He is so busy he rarely sees his three sons—leaves his office to be with them on their birthdays. Big deal. Arthur Carlsberg is no millionaire—he is a pauper." (Signed) George O. Hackett.

89. A miracle of love

In her book *Heaven in My Hand,* first-grade teacher Alice Lee Humphreys describes some of her classroom experiences. One delightful story concerns Roberta, whose father was in the Navy during World War II. Each time he was on leave, he would make it a point to bring her to school his last day at home. One particular morning he rode her to school piggyback, then paused to say good-bye.

Apologizing that he had a cold, he kissed her lightly on her dimpled cheek instead of her lips. Roberta was disappointed. Then she performed a miracle. With her thumb and forefinger, she reached up and "caught" the kiss. Then with a pretty air of triumph, she placed in squarely on her mouth.

With abandon, children often remake the realities of life with their creative imaginations. But should this mystery be lost to adults? E.g., who says you can't see the sun on a rainy day?

Joseph, sold into Egyptian slavery by his jealous brothers, refused to take revenge in later years when they came to Egypt to buy corn from the Pharoah's granaries. "So now it was not you that sent me hither, but God" is the way Joseph explained it. "Ye thought evil against me; but God meant it unto good" (Genesis 45:8 and 50:20).

Joseph took the sting of slavery and changed it to a miracle of love!

90. Reality

"The life of every man is a diary in which he means to write one story and writes another; and his humblest hour is when he compares the volume as it is with what he hoped to make it."— James M. Barrie.

91. God's will

Joe D. Brown in his book, *Stars in My Crown,* describes an attempt to lynch a Negro man. It was right after the Civil War, and his grandpa, a Methodist minister, helped save the Negro man's life. The story is a choice example of what happens when individuals in a group see themselves as they really are.

A group of angry men had gathered to hang Uncle Famous because he wouldn't sell his few acres to a greedy neighbor. As the lynching crowd gathered, Grandpa asked permission to read Uncle Famous' will:

"I ain't been able to lay much by in my life, but the things I have, I want to go to my friends. I got forty dollars in the Farmer's and Merchant's Bank and I want to leave it to Mistah Ernest Caldwell. The day he was bawn, his daddy took me in to see him, all wrinkled and red. I wanted to give him something then, but I didn't have nuthin'. I hopes he takes the forty dollars, even eff'n it is thirty years late.

"That double-barrel'd shot gun o' mine, Ah leaves to Mistah Lem Parsons. When he was a lit' boy he shot a cottontail and hit knocked him plumb over a rail fence. He's big enough and man enough to handle hit now.

"My hawgs Ah leaves to Mistah Thad Hankins. How that boy did love barbecue! Weren't hardly possible to cook hit without him comin' aroun'. Ah hopes he has a big barbecue and invites all our fren's.

Finally Grandpa came to the last page, "Ah wants all the isin' glass on mah property to go to Mistah Lon Hamilton. Mistah Hamilton wants that isin' glass pow'ful bad, and now he kin have hit. Thar is something else Ah wants to leave Mistah Hamilton. Ah wants him to have mah Bible. Hit ain't fancy Ah guess. Hit's almost wore out, but Ah wants Mistah Hamilton to have hit. Ah hopes he reads hit. Ah sure wants Mistah Perry Lokey to have my watermelon patch. He was a full-grown man 'fore he quit snitchin' mah melons and he knowed Ah seen him, too."

That was all. And Grandpa just stood there. Finally he told the men they could leave. Then one man moved forward, took the rope from Uncle's neck, and threw it down like it was dirty. The crowd dissolved. Big tears coursed down Uncle's old face. As Grandpa reached for his handkerchief, the will fell to the floor. The author tells how he stooped to pick it up, discovered it was only four blank pages. "Grandpa," he said, "this isn't a wi . . . !"

Grandpa looked down quickly. He took the four blank papers and stuffed them in his pocket. Then he smiled.

"Yes it is, son. It's the will of God."

92. Restlessness

Three common symbols characterize the restlessness of our lives. They are the herky-jerky neon sign, the can opener, and the aspirin bottle.

The flickering neon signs betray our constant search for amusement. The can opener reflects our pursuit of convenience. And the aspirin bottle indicates that to many of us, life is a splitting headache in a noisy, busy street.

93. Like anyone else

Death is the one great common denominator of human nature. We differ in so many ways during life. But death levels all of us. When Premier Joseph Stalin died in Moscow in March, 1953, American newspaper correspondent Eddy Gilmore filed a poignant story that acknowledges this fact. Here is what he cabled to American newspapers:

He was not carried to his grave in a super-plus hearse, just an ordinary looking closed body truck. It was blue. The yellow corpse in the fawn-colored, semi-military jacket. His hands stretched out stiffly, parallel with the length of his body. The rouged cheeks. The enlarged nostrils of the dictator as you looked at him from the position of his feet. Those surprisingly delicate hands and tapered fingertips. The almost scornful look of this very tough man. A look into death. His decorations lying on a silk pillow at the lower end of the coffin. The wilderness of flowers, some real, some artificial. The ebb and flow of stringed music sawed out by sweating and slightly bewildered musicians. The searing, dazzling arc lights. The slug, slug of thousands of pairs of feet passing by the bier. A tear or two. And hundreds upon hundreds of curious stares from the Russian people who couldn't get near this man when he was alive. Now they could, provided they had the strength and courage to stand long hours in long lines. But the great leveler had come by. And they saw for themselves that Joseph Stalin died just as other mortals do.

94. No substitute for love

During 1900–20, the majority of babies one-year-old and under who were placed in hospitals or orphanages never emerged alive. One United States study in 1915 showed that in ten institutions for infants, every baby under two died except one!

About the same year, Dr. Fritz Talbot visited the Children's Clinic in Dusseldorf, Germany. He was interested in what they had done to cut infant mortality.

Part of the answer he saw in a fat old woman wandering about the ward with a baby on her hip. They called her "Old Anna," and when all other treatment failed, they turned a sick child over to Anna. She literally "mothered" desperately sick children back to health. Today, medical science recognizes the value of TLC (tender loving care). And Dr. Smiley Blanton says he always protests at the sight of newborn babies in hospitals, guarded in the isolation of their sterile cribs by masked nurses. He preters to see them in cradles by their mothers' beds, or even in the arms of clumsy and apprehensive fathers.

When we talk about underprivileged children, we think of boys and girls going barefoot in winter, or eating beans for breakfast, or sleeping three or four in a lumpy bed, or dropping out of school under the fourth grade. But some underprivileged children have a dozen pairs of shoes and eat twice as much as they need: they are cold and hungry for love. Maybe they rebel and disobey and get into all kinds of trouble in the unconscious hope that someone, somewhere, will show them a little attention.

A study by Dr. Morris Rosenberg for the National Institute of Mental Health shows that even consant criticism and punishment is not necessarily the worst that could happen. Kids treated this way fare better than those whose parents just ignore them.

95. More than faultfinding

When he was told in kindergarten that he had his shoes on the wrong feet, Johnny tearfully answered, "But teacher, I haven't got any other feet!"

It is not enough to tell a fellow he is in the wrong. He probably knows that already, due to his pinched toes or pinched conscience. Unless we are willing to help a person overcome his faults, there is little value in pointing them out.

96. Noah's beard

During the Middle Ages, the Roman Catholic Church received considerable income from the display of relics. Worshipers paid to see what was claimed to be splinters and nails from the cross, the sponge lifted to the mouth of Jesus, the purple coat the mocking soldiers threw over his shoulders, thorns from his crown, the wedding ring and slippers of Mary, the carpenter tools of Jesus, the empty purse of Judas as well as his thirty pieces of silver, the perch from which the cock crew, the basin in which Herod washed his hands, manna from the desert, the beard of Noah, and even the staff of Moses!

But before we smile at the naivete with which some venerate relics, let's do a little self-examination. Ever know someone who thought so much of "the little church where I grew up" that he could never identify with any other congregation, so became a lifelong church tramp? Ever know someone who venerated "Granny's Bible," keeping it safely wrapped in plastic and stored in a trunk of heirlooms, yet never bothered to read the Sermon on the Mount, much less live by it? Ever know someone who so much admired the minister who baptized him that he could never develop loyalty to another pastor?

Then don't smile at those who carry around hairs from Noah's beard!

97. Toy trucks

Some jobs fail because they are underestimated. Like putting a band-aid on a cancer. Or prescribing sunglasses for a blind person. Or offering a starving child a stick of chewing gum. Or trying to lighten a stricken airliner by emptying the ash trays. Or attempting to gravel a ten-mile stretch of muddy road with a child's dump truck.

"For which of you, intending to build a tower, sitteth not down first, and counteth the cost, whether he have sufficient to finish it?" (Luke 14:28).

98. Bend—don't snap!

No one lives without pressure. How we take it spells success or failure. The wing of an airliner, although made of metal, has a certain amount of tolerance or give. When in flight, the wings of a huge plane actually move up and down for a distance of several feet. Otherwise, they would snap off. The rigid personality is in trouble when the going gets rough, for he has no tolerance, no elasticity, no "give." No wonder he snaps.

Robert Louis Stevenson put it this way, "Sit loosely in the saddle of life."

Isaiah 30:15 advises, "In quietness and in confidence shall be your strength."

Above all, don't follow the advice of the old limerick:

> When in trouble, when in doubt,
> Run in circles, scream and shout.

Humor sometimes relieves the pressure. Billy's mother threatened to punish him for disobedience. Scared, he ran upstairs and crawled under a bed. When his daddy came home, Billy's mother described what had happened. He went upstairs and looked under the bed for the youngster, who was still in hiding. Excitedly, Billy whispered, "What's up, Pop? Is she after you, too?"

99. Another light

Most young men who leave home to set the world on fire have to come back for more matches.

100. "Useless without you"

F. Alexander Magoun says, "Love is a passionate and abiding desire on the part of two or more people to produce together . . . an emotional climate in which each can flourish, far superior to what either could achieve alone."

And John Levy notes that an enduring marriage has one requirement: two people who are "ready to sink themselves in the creation of a new unit bigger than either of them."

So use this test on your marriage: Am I helping my husband or wife to become what she or he otherwise could never achieve alone?

This idea shines through in Rudolph Beiser's play about

Robert Browning and Elizabeth Barrett, *The Barretts of Wimpole Street*. Elizabeth, an invalid, felt unworthy of Robert's love. In reply he said, "Elizabeth, my strength needs your weakness just as much as your weakness needs my strength."

And Henry Wadsworth Longfellow echoes the same beautiful sentiments in "The Song of Hiawatha,"

> As unto the bow the cord is,
> So unto the man is woman;
> Though she bends him, she obeys him,
> Though she draws him, yet she follows;
> Useless each without the other.

101. No greater truth

The great Swiss theologian Karl Barth was meeting with a group of educators in Charlotte, North Carolina. One of the smart young professors at this meeting spoke up: "Dr. Barth, you have written many books on Christian theology. I would like to ask you, Can you put the chief message of Christianity in one sentence?"

Barth replied: "Yes, I have written many books on theology. But I can give you Christianity's answer in one sentence. This sentence is from an old song my mother used to sing to me in Switzerland when I was a child:

> Jesus loves me, this I know,
> For the Bible tells me so."

102. Laughing at yourself

We laugh easily at the foibles of others. But the ability to laugh at one's self is a helpful tension-breaker. True, life is serious. But don't take yourself too seriously. You're not an Atlas, bearing alone the weight of the world!

Abraham Lincoln is remembered as a sober, sad, and deeply reflective person. But he is also remembered for his wit and humor, including the knack of laughing at himself. Deeply hurt when he learned one of his own cabinet members called him a fool, he laughingly turned it aside. "He is a very smart man, and if he thinks I am a fool," Lincoln observed, "I had better look into the matter." The same wit was reflected when someone, poking fun at his lanky legs, asked how long a man's legs should be. "Long enough to reach the ground," Lincoln retorted.

The night Adlai Stevenson conceded the presidential election to Dwight D. Eisenhower, he called on Lincoln's wit to assuage his disappointment. In his concession speech to his weeping admirers in Springfield, Illinois, Mr. Stevenson recalled Mr. Lincoln's words on one occasion when he, too, lost an election. "I feel like a little boy who stubbed his toe in the dark. He was too big to cry, and it hurt too much to laugh."

103. The lure of adventure

Charles A. Lindbergh is famed as the first person to solo the Atlantic, on May 20–21, 1927, yet he was earlier known as "Daredevil Lindbergh." As the star of a barnstorming aerial circus, he described his first parachute jump:

I would have no pay in money for hurling my body into space. There would be no crowd to watch and applaud my landing. Nor was there any scientific objective to be gained. No, there was a deeper reason for wanting to jump, a desire I could not explain. It was a love of the air and sky, the lure of adventure, the appreciation of beauty. It lay beyond the descriptive words of men—where immortality is touched through danger, where life meets death on equal plane; where man is more than man, and existence both supreme and valueless at the same instant.

104. Not Thine, but Thee

In his book *The Meaning of Prayer,* Harry Emerson Fosdick reminds us of the chief benefit of prayer. "The great gift of God in prayer is himself, and whatever else he gives is incidental and secondary," he says. "Prayer is a cumulative life of friendship with God."

George Matheson has a beautiful prayer in which he expresses the same sentiment:

I would have my heart open at all times to receive—at morning, noon, and night; in spring, and summer, and winter. Whither Thou comest to me in sunshine or in rain, I would take Thee into my heart joyfully. Thou art Thyself more than the sunshine, Thou art Thyself compensation for the rain; it is Thee and not Thy gifts I crave; knock, and I shall open unto Thee.

Earlier in the same prayer, Matheson pleads, "I would receive even the sorrows of life as disguised gifts from thee."

"It is Thee and not Thy gifts I crave"—how many of us can sincerely offer that prayer, accustomed as we are to a gimme-gimme faith?

Thomas a Kempis (1379–1471) sounds the same note in his oft-quoted prayer:

It is too small and unsatisfying, whatsoever Thou bestowest on me apart from Thee, or revealest to me, or promisest, whilst Thou are not seen, and not fully obtained. For surely my heart cannot truly rest, nor be entirely contented, unless it rest in Thee.

105. Long-distance love

It was well known throughout the little farming community that Farmer Brown and his wife led a cat-and-dog life. Finally he built himself a cabin in a field back of the barn, moved in and left his wife the house. One day a neighbor visited him, noticed how immaculate the cabin was kept, and saw on the table a blueberry pie and a pan of freshly baked biscuits.

"Sarah comes in now and then and cleans up a bit and brings hot biscuits and such," Farmer Brown explained. "You know, no man could live with that woman, but she makes an awful good neighbor!"

106. The first step

An automobile mechanic has made a recent profession of faith in Christ. His is a dynamic, growing faith. He is enthusiastic in his desire to witness to others. How would you advise him?

Would you advise him to mount religious mottoes on the walls of his shop? or leave a soul-winning tract in the seat of cars he services? or enclose invitations to church in his monthly statements?

Perhaps. But not for his first step. His very first goal is to satisfy his customers with a job well done. He should charge a fair price, and avoid unnecessary repairs. Although some customers might never know the difference, he would refuse such gimmicks as cleaning old spark plugs while charging for new ones.

Once this service man wins the confidence and esteem of his customers, he can more readily win them to faith in Christ. And this is a basic principle for all Christians of whatever vocation, lay or clergy. If we have a way of turning people off from us, we also run the risk of turning them off from our Savior. If others don't like us, how can we expect them to like what we preach?

107. No appetite

A small boy's definition of love: "When there's only one piece of pie left, and Mother isn't hungry."

108. A tribute

An anonymous writer has given us this beautiful tribute of love, which might equally apply to family love or to friendship:

I love you not only for what you are, but for what I am when I am with you. I love you not only for what you have made of yourself, but for what you are making of me. I love you for passing over all the foolish, weak things that you can't help dimly seeing in my heart, and for drawing out into the light all the beautiful belongings that no one else had looked quite far enough to find. I love you because you are helping me to make of the lumber of my life, not a tavern but a temple and out of the works of my every day, not a reproach but a song. I love you because you have done more than any creed could have done to make me happy. You have done it without a touch, without a word, without a song. You have done it by just being Yourself.

109. The real issues?

Do church leaders meet the real needs of their people, or do too many of them waste time dusting the furniture while the house is on fire?

Jess Moody, a Baptist minister, warns that "history may record that America died because its spiritual wellsprings dried up due to the fact that the churches were fighting over the wrong issues."

Moody goes on to say: "The biggest issue we face is not all this ecclesiastical folderol . . . the gut issue is, what will the church do to keep John, Mary, Billy, and Susie Doe lashed to the cross and made into happy servants of the Lord?"

Many churches invest a great deal of energy in the conservative-liberal issue, but Moody claims that most such issues are eventually settled on the basis of "our glands instead of our brains."

He also cites the endless ecumenical-independent conflicts, but points out that neither ecumenical Christianity nor Lone Ranger-ism has remedied many real problems.

"While we have resolved, resoluted, amended, and whereas-ed, wrestling with theological issues . . . Bob, Mary, Sally, and Billy have gone without any sure word from the Lord," he concludes.

110. A crisis

A crisis is an elephant hanging from a cliff with its tail tied to a daisy.

111. More than signatures

What happened to the fifty-six men who signed the Declaration of Independence in 1776? Did they pay any personal price for liberty, or did they merely lend their signatures?

Nine died in the Revolutionary War. Five were captured by the British as traitors, and tortured before they died. Twelve had their homes ransacked and burned. Two lost sons in the War.

Carter Braxton of Virginia, a wealthy planter and trader, saw his ships swept from the seas by the British navy. He sold his home and properties to pay his debts and died in rags.

Vandals or soldiers, or both, looted the properties of Ellery, Clymer, Hall, Walton, Gwinnett, Heyward, Rutledge, and Middleton.

When his home was taken over by the British General Cornwallis at the Battle of Yorktown, Thomas Nelson, Jr. quietly urged Gen. George Washington to open fire, which he did. Nelson's home was destroyed, and he died bankrupt.

The British arrested the wife of Francis Lewis, and she died in prison.

John Hart was driven from his wife's deathbed, and their thirteen children fled for their lives.

In support of the Declaration, the fifty-six signers pledged three things: "our lives, our fortunes, and our sacred honor." Some paid with the first two, but none lost their honor.

112. Poor help

Ralph was head over heels in trouble, but doing little to help himself.

A friend advised, "Ralph, you've got two hands, why don't you do something?"

"Yes," Ralph replied, "and I'm wringing both of them!"

113. "Does death hurt?"

In her book *Beyond Our Selves,* Catherine Marshall describes a conversation with a Mrs. MacDonald, who had lost a teenage son, Kenneth, to diabetes, just months before insulin was discovered.

Mrs. MacDonald told of that day when, for the first time,

Kenneth suspected he was going to die. "Mother, what is it like to die?" he had asked. "Mother, does it hurt?"

The distraught mother told how she almost ran to the kitchen, where, leaning against a cabinet, her knuckles pressed hard against the cold, smooth surface, she prayed, "God, what can I tell him?"

God did tell her. And she in turn told Kenneth: "You remember how when you were a tiny boy, you used to play so hard all day that when night came, you would be too tired to undress? So you would tumble into Mother's bed and fall asleep?

"That was not your bed. It was not where you belonged. And you would only stay there for a little while. In the morning—to your surprise—you would wake and find youself in your own bed."

Mrs. MacDonald went on to explain to Kenneth that he would be in his own room because his father, who loved him, came with strong arms and carried him away.

Then she concluded, "So Kenneth, death is like that. We just wake up some morning to find ourselves in another room. We shall be there, because God loves us even more than our human fathers and takes care of us just as tenderly."

114. A guide to prayer

In his book *No Common Task,* George Reindrop describes the prayer habits of a nurse. Accustomed to working with her hands, she developed a prayer routine, using her fingers as a guide. Here is how it worked.

Each finger stood for someone. Her thumb, being nearest to her body, reminded her to pray for those near and dear, such as relatives and close friends. The second, or pointer finger, was a symbol of those who direct and manage, and it reminded her to pray for those who were her supervisors. The third finger, the tallest, stood for those in high positions of leadership or government.

When she looked at her fourth finger, the weakest, she remembered to pray for those who suffer from illness, disappointment, or grief. The little finger, smallest of all, she took to represent herself. Thus with meekness and humility, she expressed her own needs last of all.

115. A second start

Thomas A. Edison's son, Charles, describes the night in which his father's entire laboratory at Menlo Park burned. The famous inventor was then sixty-seven, and the winter wind blew his sparse white hair as he stood watching years of work go up in flames.

"My heart ached for him," Charles said. "He was no longer a young man. But then he spotted me and shouted, 'Charles, go find your mother. Bring her here. She'll never see anything like this as long as she lives!' "

And the next morning Thomas A. Edison observed, "There is great value in disaster. All our mistakes are burned up. Thank God we can start anew."

116. Thoughts at dying

When Monica, the mother of St. Augustine, lay dying far from home, she said to friends about her, "Bury my body where you want, for nowhere is far from God."

Edwin B. Frost, the blind astronomer who worked so brilliantly at the Yerkes Observatory, refused to succumb to fear as he approached death. At his bedside, a friend who knew his courage, asked, "Doctor, you are facing the unknown now. What does it mean? Are you afraid?" Frost smiled and shook his head, "I have seen too many stars to be afraid of the night."

O. Henry, the short-story genius, said, "Nurse, light me a candle if you please; I am afraid to go home in the dark."

Even Robert Ingersoll, the noted skeptic, in his "Oration at His Brother's Grave," said, "From the voiceless lips of the unreplying dead there comes no word; but in the night of death hope sees a star, and listening love can hear the rustle of a wing."

Albert Camus described autumn as "a second spring when every leaf's a flower."

"But it shall come to pass, that at evening time it shall be light." (Zech. 14:7).

117. God, Himself

The first public rendition of George Frederick Handel's *The Messiah* was in Dublin, Ireland, on April 13, 1742.

After the performance, someone asked Handel how he felt while composing the "Hallelujah Chorus," that climactic part when the listening audience traditionally stands to its feet.

Handel replied, "I did think I did see all heaven open before me, and the great God himself." When Lord Kinnoul complimented the entertainment he had given the town, Handel said, "I should be sorry if I only entertained. I wish to make them better."

When the curtains of heaven are pulled back and we see God in all his glory, not only are we better, but we sing and write better songs, and we desire to make others better, too.

118. Success in ten words

An old legend from Babylon describes a very rich man by the name of Arkad. He was noted for his charities, generosity with his own family, and liberalities in his own spending. Yet his wealth increased more rapidly than he spent it. His friends persuaded him to share his secret. It was found in ten words: "A part of all you earn is yours to keep."

Arkad explained that an overlooked secret of financial success is simply to live on less than you earn. One does not necessarily increase his standard of living by increasing his wealth, for if his spending grows as rapidly as his earning, he never breathes easily. Thus, absolute poverty is never abolished. The more you make, the more you want.

"Enjoy life while you are here," Arkad advised. "Do not over-strain or try to save too much. If one tenth is as much as you can comfortably keep, be content to keep this portion. Live otherwise according to your income and let not yourself get niggardly and afraid to spend. Life is good and life is rich with things worthwhile and things to enjoy."

119. One word sermon

When Roy C. DeLamotte was chaplain at Paine College in Augusta, Georgia, he preached the shortest sermon in the college's eighty-year history.

However, he had a rather long topic. It was, "What Does Christ Answer When We Ask: Lord, What's in Religion for Me?"

The complete content of his sermon was one word: "Nothing."

He explained later that the one-word sermon was meant for people "brought up on the gimme-gimme gospel." When asked how long it took him to prepare the message, Dr. DeLamotte replied, "Twenty years."

120. The true Bread

A visitor to a farm cooperative in Russia asked a gnarled Ukranian how the new communism compared with the old days.

The Ukranian answered that in the old days they invited the priests to bless the fields in the spring. "But we don't need the priests anymore," he explained, "because we have tractors now."

One need not go to Russia to find this line of reasoning. It can be found among any people who feel that if you have fertilizer, you don't need faith, that if you have penicillin, you don't need prayer, that if you have psychotherapy, you don't need salvation, that if you have social welfare, you don't need the church, and that if you have education, you don't need God.

Such shallow faith forgets that man cannot live by bread alone, and that a disease-free, hungerless generation would still starve without the Bread of Life and still thirst without the Water of Life.

121. Like a beggar

Simone Weil, in *Waiting on God,* says, "If we remain deaf, he [God] comes back again and again like a beggar, but also, like a beggar, one day he stops coming."

122. "Do you know Him?"

E. K. Judy, a Baptist minister, describes an experience that happened to him in Lexington, Kentucky.

"It was a bitter, cold January night," he recalls, "and I was waiting for a bus. Nearby was a Negro woman with a shopping bag, waiting too. I noticed that she rather nervously shifted the bag from one hand to another, but I thought she did so to keep warm. After a few minutes she took a hesitant step closer. Then she asked, almost apologetically, 'Sir, I don't mean to give no offense. But I have just been wondering, sir, do you know my Lord?' "

Christians often take courses on soul-winning, and memorize steps and procedures in witnessing. But you can hardly improve on the example of this woman, who had such an overflow of enthusiasm for her Lord that she could not keep silent, however undiplomatic her approach may have been or however inopportune the occasion.

Her testimony resembles that of Job, "I have heard of thee by the hearing of the ear: but now mine eye seeth thee" (Job 42:5).

123. High hopes

A county in the mountains of western North Carolina decided it was about time to replace the old jail building, which was about to fall down anyway. So the Board of Supervisors got together and voted three resolutions:

1. To tear down the old jail.

2. To build a new jail out of materials salvaged from the old jail.

3. But to continue using the old jail until the new one was completed!

124. Christ to me

C. H. Spurgeon, who was born in 1834 in England, is remembered primarily as a pulpiteer. He filled the Metropolitan Tabernacle in London every Sunday for over thirty years. His listeners included everyone from Queen Victoria (in disguise) on down. Once each quarter, he asked the regular members to stay home so visitors could find seats. At one time he turned down an offer of $100,000 to give 100 lectures in the United States. In addition to his fame as a preacher, he also wrote some poems, one of which is a moving testimony of his faith in Christ:

> What the hand is to the lute,
> What the breath is to the flute,
> What is fragrance to the smell,
> What the spring is to the well,
> What the flower is to the bee,
> That is Jesus Christ to me.

> What's the mother to the child,
> What the guide in pathless wild,
> What is oil to troubled wave,
> What is ransom to the slave,
> What is water to the sea,
> That is Jesus Christ to me.

125. The power of persistence

A unique experiment involving a long, heavy steel bar and a tiny bottle cork revealed the power of persistence.

In the experiment, the heavy bar was suspended on a slender steel chair from a high ceiling. Near it hung a cork weighing only four grams, suspended by a thin silk thread. The cork was pulled back, then released to hit the heavy bar. Nothing happened.

This was repeated over and over, in a rhythmic pattern. After

an hour or so, the steel bar still hung motionless. But then it
was noticed to tremble a tiny bit. The cork continued to strike.
Then with a sort of convulsive shudder, the steel bar began the
same slow, rhythmic swing as the cork. The swaying of the cork
was stopped, but the steel bar now swung back and forth, pendu-
lum-like, under its own weight.

The principle is the same as the relentless drip, drip, drip of
water which eventually wears away a rock. If one has patience,
regardless of how small his efforts, he can eventually make a
dent on life, whether it is an inaminate steel bar or the seeming
inflexible attitudes of indifferent people.

126. Easy does it

Don't make yourself—let yourself!

127. Who, not what

A wife was beginning to feel that all her efforts to win her
husband to Christ were in vain. She wondered why she was
making so little headway. "Then," she said, "I came to my
senses when, at last, my husband looked at me and shouted, 'I
certainly don't want what you have!' "

Although he was the one she most longed to reach for Christ,
at that moment she saw that her religious ways were repulsive
to him. She noticed that he didn't shout, "I don't want *who* you
have," but didn't want *what* she had.

She saw that she had been trying too hard to win him over
to her *practice of* Christianity, rather than revealing the *presence*
of Christ in her life.

If we were more careful about the Who of faith, others might
find our ways more attractive, too.

128. The two faces of worship

Worship can be objective or subjective. It can turn inward
or outward. This is illustrated by comparing the Gloria Patri with

a popular gospel song, "O That Will Be Glory."

Here is the Gloria Patri, which focuses attention on the Godhead, attributing the glory to God:

> Glory be to the Father,
> and to the Son,
> and to the Holy Ghost;
> As it was in the beginning,
> is now, and ever shall be,
> world without end. Amen, Amen.

Now compare the gospel song, which focuses attention on self and the glory to be personally enjoyed:

> When all my labors and trials are o'er,
> And I am safe on that beautiful shore,
> Just to be near the dear Lord I adore,
> Will thro' the ages be glory for me.
>
> O that will be glory for me,
> Glory for me, glory for me . . . .

The gospel song is a worthy testimony of hope and trust. But still, the emphasis is on the glory "for me."

The best worship is God-centered, using prayers that have a minimum of the personal, possessive pronouns.

129. Using what you have

The late General Douglas MacArthur, who headed the brilliant Pacific campaign during World War II, stated his philosophy in a few short words, emphasizing *action* in the *present* tense:

It doesn't matter how much you have, so long as you fight with what you have. It doesn't matter where you fight, so long as you fight. Because where you fight, the enemy has to fight too, and even though it splits your forces, it must split his force also. So fight, on whatever the scale, whenever and wherever you can. There is only one way to win victories. Attack, attack, attack!

130. Be specific

Prayer can be so general as to be meaningless ("Lord, bless all the sick . . . Bless all for whom it is our duty to pray . . . Help everyone to do right").

Wallace E. Johnson, president of Holiday Inns of America, is best known for developing the world's largest chain of motels. Often overlooked is the fact that he built more than 1,000 low-rent houses a year for at least twenty years. His habit is to make a daily list of things to pray for. On January 1, 1945, when he was getting his start, Mr. Johnson wrote this prayer:

God, please, let us build 2,000 units in 1945, and if it be in accordance with Thy divine purpose, let us accumulate enough money in that time to carry on our business. O Lord, help us to build a good house, an inexpensive house for both white and Negro citizens that has never been available to them before. And God, please, oh, please help us to convince the bankers and businessmen of our community that these are safe investments, so that we can go on an on and on. Amen.

That year, Mr. Johnson built 3,000 units and ended the year with $450,000 in the bank.

"But God never answered a prayer like that for me," we complain. But did we ever ask him? Are we specific? Do we put it in black and white? Do we really want an answer, expect an answer, and look for an answer?

"For every one that asketh receiveth; and he that seeketh findeth; and to him that knocketh it shall be opened" (Matt. 7:8).

131. The misplaced comma

I once read a sermon title, "To Hell, with God." The topic was meant to shock and catch attention, because the average person would interpret it to mean, "To hell with God." But on that comma hinges a significant insight.

If one omits the comma, as far as his experience with God is concerned, it is the same as saying that he has no use, no place, no confidence for God in his life.

But if he inserts the comma, it is his way of saying that wherever life leads, he expects to find God there. This is the meaning of Psalm 139:8–10: "If I ascend up into heaven, thou art there: if I make my bed in hell, behold, thou art there. If I take the wings of the morning, and dwell in the uttermost parts of the sea; Even there shall thy hand lead me."

The trustful, confident soul punctuates the sentence with a comma. The faithless, bitter soul omits the comma. Who could believe that one little punctuation mark could mean so much?

132. He shrieked louder

On February 13, 1843, Dr. Oliver Wendell Holmes, professor of anatomy at Harvard University, read a paper before the Boston Society for Medical Improvement that has become a milestone in medical research. The title was "The Contagiousness of Puerperal Fever," and medical historian Henry R. Viets says it "was the most important contribution made in America to the advancement of medicine."

Early nineteenth-century hospitals in Europe and America were chambers of horrors. The death rate from operations ranged from 25 to 40 percent, and considerably higher for amputations. Few medical men recognized that lack of sanitation might be responsible. Surgical instruments were cleaned only casually. Surgeons carried silk threads used for stitches in their pockets, and held operating knives with their teeth. A surgeon's coat, covered with stains and blood, was seldom if ever washed. Few doctors bothered to wash their hands when going from one patient to another or even from an autopsy to surgery.

Especially hazardous was puerperal fever, or "child-bed fever." In one of the largest hospitals in Paris, more than half of the maternity cases died.

It was Dr. Holmes' paper that aroused widespread recognition that the fever was contagious and that doctors were responsible for carrying it. His paper, reprinted in pamphlet form, is credited with saving more lives than any other single publication of the nineteenth century.

Holmes made no great claim to originality. But it was his persuasiveness, his literary style as a writer, that brought the problem to the forefront. Later, toward the end of his life, he was to write that "others had cried out with all their might against the terrible evil before I did, and I gave them full credit for it. But I think I shrieked my warning louder and longer than any of them."

Which tells us that possession of a truth is not enough. We must share the truths we know, and we must do so with conviction and urgency, even as Dr. Holmes who shrieked "louder and longer than any of them."

133. All the same

Writing in the August, 1970, issue of *Reader's Digest,* Ruth Bell describes the longtime custom in her village of the Methodists and Presbyterians holding joint services during the summer months. Each summer they would alternate the building in which they worshiped. And to avoid confusion, the congregation would use the form of the Lord's Prayer which was customary to the host church.

She recalls one summer, when the Sunday came for the final joint service. The presiding minister announced, "The time has now come for the Methodists to return to their trespasses and leave the Presbyterians to their debts."

134. Nature's power

One of the most awesome spectacles of nature is a summer thunderstorm, which can release as much as a hundred thousand tons of rain and generate winds up to 70 miles per hour. At any given moment, about 1,800 thunderstorms are going on throughout the world. In the United States, the West Coast experiences the fewest thunderstorms—less than ten a year. But Florida, which is buffeted by more than 100 a year, is the thunderstorm capital of the nation.

A thunderhead may peak as high as 40,000 feet, and along with the deluge of water may come hail as big as tennis balls. The biggest hailstone on record measured 17 inches in circumference and fell at Potter, Nebraska, on July 6, 1928.

To many people, lightning is the most terrifying feature of a storm, yet it has a beauty and function all its own. A streak of lightning may be as short as 300 feet, or in extreme cases, flashes 20 miles in length have been measured. In a cloud to earth flash, the lightning travels from 100 to 1,000 miles per second on the down stroke, and reaches up to 87,000 miles per second (almost half the speed of light) for the return stroke. And every few million strokes, there is a giant discharge from and to the top of a thunderhead. In these "positive giants," energy up to 3 billion joules is sometimes recorded. And the temperature of those super-flashes is about 30,000° C., more than five times as hot as the sun's surface.

Although it is not commonly known, lightning frees nitrogen from the air, and rain washes it into the soil at the rate of 100 million tons a year—and it is thus a valuable and free source of fertilizer. Another by-product has never been tapped—electrical energy. One large storm creates enough electricity to power a large city for several days. But its energy is wasted, because man has not learned to harness it.

Here is a parable of life. We waste far more than we use, whether the resources of nature or the resources of personality. If we could use just one tenth of the energy we waste envying others to develop our own native abilities, we would surprise even ourselves with what we accomplished.

135. Good at heart?

It is commonly said that "all people are good at heart." But are they? Jeremiah 17:9 says that the "heart is deceitful above all things, and desperately wicked: who can know it?"

In the summer of 1970, the state of Delaware experimented with the honor system for twenty days on the Delaware Turnpike.

Motorists without exact change at the automatic toll booths were allowed to take return envelopes and mail in the money.

But in twenty days, of more than 26,000 envelopes taken, only 582 were returned, according to the Associated Press. And of those that were returned, some had stamps and pieces of paper instead of money. The experiment cost the state about $4,000 before it was discontinued. And that didn't include lost tolls.

136. You are what you think

Angelo Siciliano (popularly known as Charles Atlas, "the world's most perfectly developed man") was born of Italian immigrant parents in Brooklyn. He grew up in the slums as a scrawny, thin, undernourished lad. At sixteen he weighed only ninety-seven pounds. A pale, nervous runt, he was an easy prey for bullies. Then one day in the lobby of the Brooklyn Museum, he became entranced with the statues of the Greek gods, especially Hercules. He could hardly believe these powerful statues had been posed by men. So he decided to make himself over in the likeness of a Greek god. He had no fancy gym equipment, but he clipped a series of exercises from a newspaper and devised his own system for tensing one muscle against the other.

It was hard work. Other boys made fun. Bue he was determined. And eventually the skinny runt from Brooklyn became known as Charles Atlas, described as a man of "true classic physique, in perfect proportions."

If you ever visit the statue of Alexander Hamilton in front of the Treasury Building in Washington, D.C., or the statue of George Washington in the Washington Square monument in New York City, remind yourself that Charles Atlas posed for the sculptor.

The late William James is perhaps best noted for his insight that by changing one's attitude toward himself, he can actually change himself. Proverbs 23:7 said the same truth centuries ago, "For as he thinketh in his heart, so is he."

137. Children and smoking

According to an article in the Detroit *Free Press* by Bob Talbert, children are the best weapons in the world against smoking parents.

Talbert cites three examples of well-known mothers who quit smoking at the insistence of their children, who in turn had been influenced by anti-smoking commercials. One is Jacqueline Onassis, who is reported to have dropped smoking at the insistence of her daughter, Caroline Kennedy.

When Patti Page's children, at the ages of six and seven, asked their mother to quit, Patti gave up her two packs a day. And when Carol Burnett's daughter, Carrie, was four, she saw Carol light up a cigarette one day and asked, "Mommie, don't you want to see me grow up?"

Considerate parents will do almost anything which they feel will benefit their children. And best of all, when parents do something good for their boys and girls, they inevitably wind up doing something good for themselves!

138. Power of words

The boast that one picture is worth a thousand words is debatable. Well-chosen words stir the soul, fire the imagination, and stimulate to action.

Such were the words of Thomas Paine who played a major role in inspiring the American Revolution, had a direct hand in drafting the Declaration of Independence, and helped maintain the morale of George Washington's army at its lowest ebb.

He is best known for his book *Common Sense,* published anonymously as an eighty-page pamphlet. It first appeared in Philadelphia on January 10, 1776. Within three months, 120,000 copies had been sold, and total sales may have reached one-half million copies. This made it the American best seller of all time in relation to population, which was then about two and one-half million. After reading *Common Sense,* Major General Lee wrote to George Washington that it would "give the *coup-de-grace* to Great Britain."

During the Revolutionary War, General Washington asked Paine to write a series of papers entitled *The American Crisis,* designed to inspire the troops and hearten the citizenry. These papers were almost universally read in the colonies and helped keep the struggle for independence alive when it seemed headed for disaster. The opening paragraph of the first *Crisis* shows the power of words to fire the imagination:

> These are the times that try men's souls. The summer soldier and the sunshine patriot will, in this crisis, shrink from the service of their country; but he that stands it *now* deserves the love and thanks of man and woman. Tyranny, like hell, is not easily conquered; yet we have this consolation with us, that the harder the conflict, the more glorious the triumph.

In issuing a call to discipleship, Christ showed the same ability to challenge the best in a person through words: "If any man will come after me, let him deny himself, and take up his cross, and follow me. For whosoever will save his life shall lose it: and whosoever will lose his life for my sake shall find it" (Matt. 16:24–25).

139. Sallman's Head of Christ

The late Warner E. Sallman is known the world over for his famous painting, *Head of Christ.* Over 150 million reproductions have been sold in more than fifty countries.

Sallman developed a life philosophy during a near-brush with death from tuberculosis: "When we turn our lives over to God, without reservation, he can and will do remarkable things through us." Note the phrase, "through us," for that became his motto.

Sallman painted the *Head of Christ* in 1924, largely on the inspiration he received at a series of Bible talks at the Chicago Central YMCA. The painting began as an assignment for a magazine cover. He had struggled with the drawing for days and days, but lacked that spark of inspiration. The night before the magazine cover was due, he prayed for an inspiration, for God to work "through him." The answer came. About two o'clock in the morning he saw "a clear, beautiful image of Christ." Lest he forget the image, he rushed to his attic studio and made a thumbnail sketch, which he finished the next morning.

Not everyone can become a famous artist, or a famous anything. But each can submit himself to the creative power of God, allowing the Divine to do his perfect work with imperfect humanity.

140. Love isn't soft

Ephesians 4:15 lists the ability to speak "the truth in love" as one sign of Christian maturity. This is a two-way street. Because we love someone doesn't keep us from telling them the truth, even when it hurts. On the other hand, "telling it like it is" doesn't require that we be mean in the way we say it.

This was illustrated at the Billy Graham Crusade in Knoxville, Tennessee, in the summer of 1970, attended by President and Mrs. Richard M. Nixon. Who received the biggest ovation that night—the President, or Billy? Neither! It was the seventy-year-old singer, actress, and TV personality, Ethel Waters.

Here's how it happened. Demonstrators were chanting obscenities. As Ethel stood to sing, she said to them, "I love you, children, but if I was over there where you are, I'd just smack you. But I love you and I'd also give you a big hug and kiss and tell you so." The hecklers fell silent, and the rest of the 75,000 people in the University of Tennessee stadium gave their biggest ovation of the evening. Ethel spoke the truth, but she spoke it in love. This is surely the meaning of Ephesians 4:14–15, "That we henceforth be no more children, tossed to and fro . . . but speaking the truth in love, may grow up . . ."

141. Holding grudges

Imagine, if you can, a fellow swinging from the limb of a tree. His hands are clinched and drawn as if he were chained to the limb. All of his clothing has long since rotted and fallen off. His body is dirty, emaciated, and weatherworn. "Why don't you turn loose and come down?" You shout to the strange, mad-like creature swinging in the wind.

"Oh," he replies, "about twenty years ago a flash flood swept through this valley, and to save my life, I reached up and grabbed this limb."

"And you've been hanging there ever since, for twenty years?" you ask in shocked disbelief. Then you learn that this was such a traumatic experience for this person that he could never force himself to turn loose. And there he had swayed in the wind, back and forth, for twenty years.

An impossible story? Certainly. No man could hold on to a limb for twenty weeks or even twenty days without food and water. But it *is* possible for a man to hold on to an old grudge for twenty or even forty years or longer.

Long after everyone else has forgotten, he nurses some real or imagined wrong in his heart. He is emotionally starved, spiritually naked, and psychologically bruised. So there he swings in the wind, crippled by old grudges that others have long since forgotten.

A ninety-two-year-old woman once said to me, "I never let the sun go down on a grudge. I don't carry my troubles forward to the next day. I bury the past at every sunset."

142. Unconscious influence

On one occasion, Thorwaldsen, the noted Danish sculptor, spent some time working in Italy. He brought home with him the pieces of marble sculptures that made him famous. As the servants unpacked the marbles, they scattered on the ground the straw in which they came packed.

The next summer, flowers from the gardens of Rome were blooming in the streets of Copenhagen, from the seeds thus borne in the straw and planted by accident. While breathing life into cold marble, Thorwaldsen was at the same time unconsciously scattering other beautiful things to give cheer and gladness.

So all day long, we who are Christ's workers may unconsciously bless the world. As we go about our routine tasks, we can drop gentle words from our lips and scatter little seeds of kindness about us. And tomorrow, flowers from the garden of God will spring up in the dusty streets of earth and along the hard paths where our fellowmen walk.

143. Living heroes

Monuments are often erected to the memory of heroes who give their lives, and public buildings are named in their honor. But we are not so quick to honor a person who *lives* for a cause as we are one who *dies* for a cause. Yet a daily, living sacrifice may take more courage than a moment of blazing glory that ends in death.

Immolation (suicide by fire) was a popular means of protest during the Vietnam War, both in Vietnam and in the United States. Within a one-week period in November, 1965, two young Americans set fire to themselves. Norman Morrison burned himself to death outside the Pentagon in Washington, and Roger LaPorte doused his clothes with gasoline and set himself aflame on a street corner outside the United Nations in New York City. In commenting on self-imposed martyrdom, psychoanalyst Wilhelm Stekel once said, "The mark of an immature man is that he wants to die nobly for a cause, while the mark of the mature man is that he wants to live humbly for one."

This is not denying the need for and courage involved in giving one's life. But it *is* magnifying the importance of daily, persistent, unsung devotion to something one believes in devotedly.

Paul made such a plea for dedicated Christians when he said, "I beseech you therefore . . . that ye present your bodies a living sacrifice . . . which is your reasonable service" (Rom. 12:1).

144. Late starts

"Head Start" was a popular program during the 60's and later to provide preschool learning experience for deprived children.

But a "Middle Start" and a "Late Start" emphasis is also needed to help our aging population find meaning for their lives.

By 1970, there were twenty million Americans sixty-five or over. They have jumped, proportionately, from 2.5 percent of the nation's population in 1850 to 10 percent today.

One of the major tragedies of the twentieth century could be the large numbers of older people who feel life no longer has significance, that they are neither wanted nor needed. Psychiatrist Robert Butler predicts that in twenty-five or thirty years, age-ism will be a problem equal to racism. One elderly man lamented, "There is no one still alive who can call me John."

Butler also warns that "perhaps the greatest danger in life is being frozen into a role that limits one's self-expression and development.

One answer is to restore purpose, regardless of one's age. But how? Much depends on the attitude of the individual. Carl Jung, who lived with great vigor to eighty-five, said, "From the middle of life onward, only he remains vitally alive who is ready to die with life, for in the secret hour of life's midday, the parabola is reversed, death is born. We grant goal and purpose to the ascent of life, why not to the descent?" Erik Erickson echoes the same sentiments: "Any span of the cycle lived without vigorous meaning, at the beginning, in the middle, or at the end, endangers the sense of life and the meaning of death . . ."

A good example is Mrs. Florida Scott-Maxwell, who at fifty began training as a psychotherapist. In her book *The Measure of My Days,* she shares her ideas about aging. "My seventies were interesting and fairly serene, but my eighties are passionate. I am so disturbed by the outer world, and by human quality in general, that I want to put things right as though I still owed a debt to life."

The key may be interest in the "outer world." When persons of any age grow preoccupied with the "inner world" of self, life has a way of turning sour. In the words of Dylan Thomas:

> Old age should burn and
> rave at close of day.

145. Hands of friendship

An old Oriental proverb asks, "We know the sound of two hands clapping, but who has heard the sound of one hand clapping?"

Likewise, did you ever try to wash, using only one hand? Not so simple, is it? It is when we bring two hands together that we clap, and when we rub two hands together that we get them clean.

Just as we join our hands to perform everyday tasks, so we join hands with others to do what we could never do alone. And in the same sense, we join hands with God, as one of B. B. McKinney's well-known hymns suggests, "Place your hand in the nail-scarred hand." When Moses complained that he could not lead the Israelites to safety, God asked, "What is that in thine hand?" (Ex. 4:2). Each of us holds within our hands some talent for service.

Doubtless you are familiar with Albrecht Durer's famous painting, *Praying Hands*. The two hands, arched in prayer, are those of an older man. They are toil-worn and scarred. The fingernails are broken, the joints enlarged. Durer, a German painter, was too poor to study painting. He lived with a friend, who also aspired to be an artist, but they could not make it financially. Finally, his friend suggested that since Durer was the younger and more talented, he should spend his entire time studying and painting. Meanwhile, his friend washed dishes and scrubbed floors in a restaurant. By the time Durer was an established painter with a regular income, his friend was too old and his fingers too twisted for him to paint. One day Durer returned to the room unexpectedly to find his friend in prayer, his work-worn hands folded reverently. These hands were the inspiration for the well-known painting.

What is in *your* hand?

146. Big order

Christian love is to will the well-being of the whole being of every being.

147. Christ as a daily presence

The late F. Townley Lord was president of the Baptist World Alliance from 1950 to 1955, editor of *The Baptist Times,* and longtime pastor of the Bloomsbury Baptist Church in London. A collection of his editorials in essay form are in his book, *The Faith That Sings.*

In one of the essays, he reminisces about his parents, who lived during the Victorian Era, and were active lay people in the Baptist work in Great Britain. His father he describes as a simple working man, who as a lay teacher and preacher spent long hours studying the Bible. When he comes to describe his mother, one sentence is pregnant with meaning: "She knew nothing of the discussions of the scholars about the Saviour as a historic figure, but everything of him as a daily Presence."

The Christian faith, in the final analysis, is not something to be debated or proven, but an experience of faith with a Person. Without the Person, all arguments are meaningless. With the Person, arguments are unnecessary.

148. "Just married or somethin' "

Parents are often confused by conflicting theories on how to rear children. Should they be permissive or authoritarian? Should they go by child psychology or woodshed physiology?

What goals are most important—to see that kids get enough to eat, benefit from a good education, have a lot of fun while growing up, inherit a fortune at twenty-one, live in a nice neighborhood, go to church regularly, or make the right kind of friends?

At the risk of oversimplification, here is priority number 1: The best thing a father can do for his son is to love that boy's mother. And the best thing a mother can do for her daughter is to love her father.

When children grow up in a loveless home where constant tension is the daily menu, they are sure to feel a false guilt that asks . . . "What did I do wrong?". . . "Am I the cause of all this?" . . . "Would Mother and Daddy have been better off without me?"

In his book *Promises to Peter,* Charlie W. Shedd quotes an eleven-year-old boy fortunate enough to have parents who love each other:

> My mother keeps a cookie jar in the kitchen, and we can help ourselves except we can't if it is too close to mealtime. Only my dad can any time. When he comes home from the office, he helps himself no matter if it is just before we eat. He always slaps my mother on the behind and brags about how great she is and how good she can cook. Then she turns around and they hug. The way they do it you would think they just got married or something. It makes me feel good. This is what I like best about my home.

In the same book, Shedd describes what happened when this subject came up in his own family. "Who do you love most? Us, or each other?" The Shedds replied frankly that they loved each other more than they did the children. They explained that although the love of husband and wife differs from parent-child love, the fact remains that there is no stronger love than husband-wife.

(You may find this hard to accept. But look at it this way. The more parents love each other, the greater will be their love for their children. And there is a depth of parental love which a child can never taste unless there is first an ocean-depth of father-mother love. To be a lifetime sweetheart to your husband or wife does not diminish the love enjoyed by the kids—it only enhances it).

Shedd admits he was apprehensive over what he had said. But he was later reassured by one of his children. "At first it seemed like my world was coming apart when I heard you say that. But after I thought it over, I felt like everything fit together again good."

It is unfortunate that some prudish parents who are afraid to show any affection outside the bedroom never hesitate to scatter their hostilities all over the house. (And this is not saying that the sexual is the only expression of love.)

But a wonderful trait of love is that—unlike school, clothes, food, toys, education, friends, travel, etc.—it is both age-proof and inflation-proof.

149. Had it made

Joe McCarthy, one-time manager of the New York Yankees, tells about the dream in which he died and went to heaven. There he was ordered by St. Peter to organize and manage a ball team. McCarthy says he was overwhelmed by all the available talent— Christy Mathewson, Walter Johnson, Rube Waddell, Babe Ruth, Lou Gehrig, and all the other superstars.

Just then the phone rang. It was Satan calling from downstairs to challenge the heavenly team to a game.

"But you haven't got a chance of winning," McCarthy replied. "You see, I've got all the ballplayers up here."

Satan explained, "Oh, I know that. But I've got all the umpires!"

150. Double vision

Whether in a church, the home, a community, or on the job, it is difficult for two or more people to agree on any controversial issue unless they study it together.

Far in the backwoods lived an elderly couple, Tom and Ella, who had never seen a mirror. One day Tom stumbled on to one in an old trunk in the barn loft. Looking at it, he thought the image was a picture of his father, since it so closely resembled him. Day after day Tom would return to the barn loft to gaze at his father's likeness. His wife, Ella, suspicious of his long absences, made a search of the barn loft, too. When she held the mirror before her face, she also thought it was a picture, but certainly not of her sainted father-in-law!

So that night she greeted her husband with the words, "Tom, while you were at work I opened the trunk and found that picture. I never saw such a homely old woman in my life. If you're going to waste your time looking at pictures like that, I'm through with you!"

The argument was not settled until they got the mirror and looked at it together.

151. Bless whom?

In *The War Prayer,* Mark Twain describes a community swept by patriotic enthusiasm in which the drums were beating, the bands playing, the flags waving, the firecrackers hissing, and the volunteers daily marching down the wide avenues in their new uniforms.

On Sunday morning the local church was filled, the volunteers sitting in reserved sections with "their young faces alight with martial dreams—visions of the stern advance, the gathering momentum, the rushing charge, the flashing sabers, the flight of the foe, the tumult, the enveloping smoke, the fierce pursuit, the surrender—then home from the war, bronzed heroes, welcomed, adored, submerged in golden seas of glory!"

The minister read a war chapter from the Old Testament, the first prayer was said, followed by an organ burst that shook the building, and then the congregation joining in the invocation:

> God the all-terrible! Thou who ordainest,
> Thunder thy clarion and lightning thy sword!

Next the pastoral prayer, that an ever-merciful Father would "watch over our noble young soldiers . . . aid, comfort, and encourage them . . . shield them in the day of battle . . . make them strong and confident, invincible in the bloody onset; help them to crush the foe, grant to them . . . imperishable glory . . . ."

From the back an ageless stranger made his way down the main aisle, touched the minister's arm, and asked him to step aside. He reminded the congregation that by praying for rain on their crops which need it, it is possible they were praying for a curse upon some neighbor's crop which did not need rain and might be injured by it.

He went on to say that their prayer for military victory might have meant, unintentionally, the following:

"O Lord . . . help us to tear their soldiers to bloody shreds with our shells . . . to cover their smiling fields with the pale forms of their patriotic dead . . . to drown the thunder of the guns with the shrieks of their wounded . . . to lay waste their humble homes with a hurricane of fire . . . to wring the hearts of their unoffending widows with unavailing grief . . . to turn them out roofless with their little children to wander in rags and hunger and thirst . . . For our sakes, blast their hopes, blight their lives . . . make heavy their steps, water their way with their tears, stain the white snow with the blood of their wounded feet . . . in the spirit of Him who is the Source of love . . . Amen."

It was believed afterward that the unannounced visitor was a lunatic since there was no sense in what he said, or what he prayed.

152. A better way

A sheepman in Indiana was troubled by his neighbor's dogs who were killing his sheep. He considered a number of possibilities, such as a lawsuit, a new barbed-wire fence, or even the use of his shotgun.

Finally he settled on a better idea. He gave to every neighbor child a lamb or two as pets. In due time, when all his neighbors had their own small flocks they began to tie up their dogs, and that solved the problem.

153. How to succeed

Looking for a sure-fire formula for success, in almost any field? Here it is, in eight simple words: surround yourself with people smarter than you are.

Compare this spirit with the individual who can never stand to work around anyone who knows more than he does. Unfortunately, the inability to recognize excellence in others may creep into churches. The pastor who feels he must excel every staff member. The minister of music who cannot tolerate a choir member who sings better than he. The deacon chairman who is suspicious of any deacon who seems to have more influence than he.

Writing in *Forbes* magazine, H. S. Burns said: "A good manager is a man who isn't worried about his own career but rather the careers of those who work for him. Take care of those who work for you, and you'll float to greatness on their achievements."

154. Knots and lemons

Everyone has his share of disappointments. And the deciding factor is not how big the disappointment, but how one reacts to the problem.

Julius Rosenwald, when he was chairman of the board of Sears, Roebuck and Co., used to say, "When life hands me a lemon, I make a lemonade out of it."

"When you get to the end of your rope, tie a knot and hang on" is another way of saying it.

The mother of Dwight D. Eisenhower, who was fond of solitaire, often said, "The Lord deals the cards; you play them."

And Dick Gregory's mother, when there was no fatback to go with the beans, no socks to go with the shoes, and no hope to go with tomorrow, would say to her kids, "We ain't poor, we're just broke."

Henry Ward Beecher ties this whole subject in a neat little package of twenty-three words: "God asks no man whether he will accept life. This is not the choice. You must take it. The only choice is *how*."

155. Today and tomorrow

When travelers cross a time zone, they set their watches forward or backward a mere one hour. But when crossing the International

Date Line at the 180th meridian, one must add or subtract an entire day, depending on his direction. If headed west, he adds a day. If coming east, he subtracts a day from the calendar (which means he lives the same day two times!).

Now imagine you are on a plane, flying north or south along the 180th meridian. Since it would be very difficult to navigate along an exact, imaginary line, your plane would, by a slight variance here and there, be zigzagging back and forth from today into tomorrow and back again.

In fact, when Rear-Admiral Richard E. Byrd made his second trip to the South Pole, he later reported in the *National Geographic* that it was impossible to fly along a mathematical line, although he had flown as closely as possible along the 180th meridian.

Man is the only creature who senses that there is a tomorrow. This means he can never be totally immersed in the present, knowing that tomorrow with all its uncertainties is just over the horizon. But neither can he live totally in the future, pressed as he is by the demands of today. So he zigzags between the two, and success often depends on a happy balance.

"I must work the works of him that sent me, while it is day: the night cometh, when no man can work" (John 9:4).

156. Queen of proverbs

"The road to hell is paved with good intentions."

Archbishop William Temple described this as "perhaps the queen of all proverbs."

A similar note was sounded by the senior "devil" Screwtape to his nephew, Wormwood, a junior "devil" on earth. In *The Screwtape Letters, author* C. S. Lewis makes Screwtape to say: "Indeed the safest road to Hell is the gradual one—the gentle slope, soft underfoot, without sudden turnings, without milestones, without signposts."

157. Man in peril

Frank K. Kelly wrote, "Man lives on a beautiful colored ball, traveling at high speed through enormous darkness toward the fires of countless suns."

But the "beautiful colored ball" which we call earth is in peril. Grave peril. Like Apollo 13 which limped back to earth in the spring of 1970 with dangerously low levels of oxygen, fuel, and water, so spaceship Earth is literally running out of room, food, air, and water for its burgeoning population, destined to leapfrog from the current three and one-half billion souls to seven billion by the year 2000, less than thirty years away.

The ecological crisis has two major causes: man's technological skill, and man's desire to reproduce himself.

The industrial revolution has raised the standard of living, bringing untold luxury and convenience. But technology has spawned effluence as well as affluence.

"Progress" means that to run our air-conditioners, we will strip-mine a Kentucky hillside, push the rock and slate into a nearby stream, and burn coal in a power plant whose smokestack contributes to a plume of smoke massive enough to cause cloud seeding and premature precipitation in Gulf clouds, which should be irrigating the wheat farms of Kansas.

The second cause is just too many people. Paul R. Ehrlich in his book *The Population Bomb,* says, "Too many cars, too many factories, too much detergent, too much pesticide, multiplying contrails, inadequate sewage treatment plants, too little water, too much carbon dioxide—all can be traced easily to *too many people*."

Ehrlich goes on to say that just as "a cancer is an uncontrolled multiplication of cells" so "the population explosion is an uncontrolled multiplication of people."

158. Could have been

About a year before his death, George Bernard Shaw granted one of his rare interviews to a well-known journalist. The reporter questioned the aged playwright at length.

Finally he asked: "Mr. Shaw, you have known some of the greatest men of our time: statesmen, artists, philosophers, writers, and musicians. You've now outlived most of them. Suppose it were possible for you to call back one of those great minds—which one would it be? What man do you miss the most?"

Without hesitation the biting satirist answered, "The man I miss the most is the man I used to be!"

159. The Bible and ecology

Does the Bible say anything about solving the environmental crisis?

The Old Testament says much about personal cleanliness and sanitation. Leviticus 14:8–9 gives detailed instructions for washing and shaving after illness. Exodus 29:14 tells how "the flesh of the bullock, and his skin, and his dung, shall thou burn with fire without the camp." Before God gave the Law on Mt. Sinai, he instructed the people to "wash their clothes" (Ex. 19:10). The blood of slain animals and fowl was to be covered "with dust" (Lev. 17:13).

To insure that their camps would be fit for God's presence, the Israelites were instructed to carry a trowel or paddle. "When you squat outside" the camp, orders Deuteronomy 23:13 (NEB), "you shall scrape a hole . . . and cover your excrement."

When God finished creation, he saw that "it was very good" and placed man in the garden "to dress it and to keep it" (Gen. 1:31; 2:15). This does not mean that man is to act like a hog. As Proverbs 13:22 predicts, "A good man leaveth an inheritance to his children's children." But if man exploits the earth and pollutes the atmosphere, what inheritance can he leave for his children, to say nothing of his grandchildren?

The land laws of Israel illustrate a basic principle of man's trusteeship. In Leviticus 25:1–23, God told the Jewish people to let the land rest every seventh year. (Any farmer knows how the land is depleted if planted year after year with the same crop). Also, the land was to lay idle the fiftieth year, the Jubilee. In that year all land was to revert to its original owners, and all slaves were to be freed. The price of land and slaves was set on the basis of the years remaining until the Jubilee. Property bought the fortieth year, e.g., was much cheaper than land bought the fourth year. In a sense, the land was leased for a period not to exceed forty-nine years.

"For the land is mine" is the way God expressed it in Leviticus 25:23. How rigidly the Jews observed this law in Old Testament times is not known. A return to the Year of Jubilee is not necessarily the solution. But the principle is that land is not the exclusive possession of any one generation. To deplete the soil, foul the air, or pollute the water is contrary to God's will, for this, too, is his.

160. Never satisfied

William Jennings Bryan reportedly said: "Those who live for money spend the first half of their lives getting all they can from everybody else, and the last half trying to keep everybody else from getting what they have got away from them; and they find no pleasure in either half."

When John D. Rockefeller, Sr. was asked how much money it takes to satisfy a man, he replied, "Just a little bit more!"

161. Feelings follow actions

Many years ago E. Stanley Jones observed that it is easier to *act* yourself into a new way of thinking than to *think* yourself into a new way of acting. Or stated simpler, feelings follow actions.

To feel right, one must act right!

William James affirmed this when he wrote, "Action and feeling go together, and by regulating the action, . . . we can directly regulate the feeling."

In his book, *On Being a Real Person,* Harry E. Fosdick says the same, "The physical expression of an emotion deepens and reinforces that emotion."

"Assume a virtue, if you have it not," which was Hamlet's advice to his mother, is not necessarily an approval of hypocrisy. The assumed virtue can become a virtue.

We have long recognized the effect of the mind on the body (Prov. 23:7, "As he [a man] thinketh in his heart, so is he"). But the actions of the body can also affect the thinking of the mind. As Marie Ray says in her book, *How Never to Be Tired:* "When you feel depressed, act cheerful—and soon you will feel cheerful. Square your shoulders, step out, smile; soon you'll find yourself feeling quite cheery. . . . The mere posture of the body induces a mood, even though it be consciously assumed."

Sometimes when I face an unhappy chore, I tell myself, "Don't make yourself—let yourself." Just turn your body loose to take over the job, irregardless of the feeling, and before you know it, you will be drawing on an inner emotion that makes the job downright enjoyable.

Do you want to "feel" good? Then act good. Do you want to overcome fear? Then act brave. Do you want to be well liked? Then act friendly. Do you want good health? Then act as if you felt good.

Yes, feelings follow actions!

162. Happy waters

An undernourished nine-year-old boy left the tragic living conditions of a large, poverty-ridden family to live in a foster home sponsored by Buckner Orphans Home, a Baptist institution in Texas.

His name was Eddie, and the first evening was a frightening experience. For the first time in his life he was to take a bath in a real bathtub.

Eddie was embarrassed to undress and reveal his torn, dirty underwear held together by safety pins. But his new foster mother said reassuringly, "I'll wash them out right away."

Eddie bathed, washed his hair, brushed his teeth, put on clean clothes and came out of the bathroom glistening all over.

"You know, Mom Chapman," he said, "them were the happiest waters I've ever seen in my life!"

163. He had a dream

When Neil Armstrong first set foot on the moon the night of July 20, 1969, headlines around the world screamed the exploits of the Apollo 11 mission. And Armstrong and his fellow astronauts deserved every word of praise. But this, and other space exploits, are largely due to the *dream* of a man who never lived to see a moon-landing. He was Robert H. Goddard, who pioneered in liquid-fueled rocketry, and whose first rocket climed only 41 feet when fired from a Massachusetts meadow on a gray March day in 1926. Goddard is to rocketry what the Wright brothers are to aviation, since he patented 214 devices and parts, most of them essential to the operation of modern rocket engines.

And it all started with a boyhood dream back in 1899.

Goddard recorded the dream in his diary. "On the afternoon of October 19, 1899, I climbed a tall cherry tree at the back of the barn and started to trim dead limbs. It was one of the quiet, color-ful afternoons of sheer beauty which we have in New England and as I looked toward the fields . . . I imagined how wonderful it would be to make some device which had even the *possibility* of ascending to Mars . . . . I was a different boy when I descended the tree."

Later he wrote, "When old dreams die, new ones come to take their place. God pity the one-dream man."

His widow says, "His dream couldn't change. Everything he did was aimed at the achievement of space flight."

Goddard's dream as a boy in a cherry tree reminds us of Isaiah's vision in the Temple (Isa. 6). Isaiah was never the same after seeing the Lord high and lifted up. Likewise, Goddard was never the same after his boyhood vision. Truly, as James B. O'Reilly said, "back of the job is the dreamer, making the dream come true."

Some people are content to saw dead limbs of the past. Others must break new ground and plant new trees. Whether Bobby Goddard ever finished trimming the cherry tree is unknown. What is known is that giant Saturn rockets in the 1960's blossomed from a boy's dream on an October afternoon in 1899.

"Go down the alleys that people say are blind; voyage to the worlds that people say have already been discovered: another look may make another world."—Socrates, paraphrased by Michael P. Kammer.

164. Overrated

Is one picture really worth a thousand words? Well, that depends on the picture and the thousands words.

The greatest material force in the world may be the twenty-five ten-thousandths (.0025) of an inch thickness of printer's ink applied to a page of copy. T.R. Glover said that only four words destroyed slavery, "for whom Christ died."

With just a thousand words you can write the Lord's Prayer, the twenty-third Psalm, the Hippocratic oath, a sonnet by Shakespeare, the Preamble to the U.S. Constitution, Lincoln's Gettysburg address, and still have enough words left over for the Boy Scout oath.

"Now ye are clean through the word which I have spoken unto you . . . . For I have given unto them the words which thou gavest me" (John 15:3; 17:8).

"The words that I speak unto you, they are spirit, and they are life" (John 6:63b).

165. Misuse, not use

Public reaction is mixed at any great breakthrough in history. Such was the case on July 16, 1945, when at 5:30 A.M. the atomic age was ushered in at a remote section of a New Mexico desert called Jornada del Muerto (Journey of Death). William Laurence of the New York *Times* was the only journalist to witness the world's first explosion of an atomic bomb, which took place that fateful day. Mr. Laurence later wrote how he felt—as if he had been present at the dawn of creation when God said, "Let there be light."

In contrast, physicist J. Robert Oppenheimer was reminded of a few words from the *Bhagavad-Gita,* "I am become Death, the shatterer of worlds."

One witness saw life in the detonation, while another saw death, and rightly so. For nuclear energy has the potential for either. The spilt atom is neither good nor evil—only the use to which it is put is good or bad.

This is universally true. It is the misuse of God's creation, not the use, that breeds so much heartache, suffering, and pain. In contrast with so sophisticated an element as nuclear energy, compare a simple example, plain water. Life is impossible without moisture, yet in uncontrolled quantities it can wreck utter havoc. God's world is to be used and enjoyed, not misused and destroyed.

166. Souls and soles

"The cobbler who repairs the sole of the Pope's shoe is doing a work as important as that of the Pope who saves the soul of the cobbler."—Attributed to Martin Luther.

167. The sound of music

In the history of religions, only two have developed the art of music as an integral part of worship—Judaism and Christianity. In all other religions, we find the dirge and the chant. And Christianity has far outstripped Judaism in music of praise and adoration.

"There will be no singing" appeared on the printed notices announcing the funeral services of the noted unbeliever, Robert Ingersoll. This was fitting, for what was there to sing about?

The sound of music echoes throughout the Scriptures. After crossing the Red Sea on dry land, Moses and the Israelites burst out with, "I will sing unto the Lord, for he hath triumphed gloriously" (Ex. 15:1).

A choir of 4,000 plus 300 instrumentalists "with shouting, and with sound of the cornet, and with trumpets, and with cymbals, making a noise with psalteries and harps" were used when David moved the ark of the covenant to the tabernacle (1 Chron. 15:28).

Heavenly choirs announced the birth of Jesus. He and his disciples sang a hymn at the Last Supper. Paul and Silas, beaten and locked in stocks in a Philippian jail, sang praises at midnight. And exiled on the Isle of Patmos, John heard beautiful music "as the voice of many waters" and "as the voice of a great thunder," together with "the voice of harpers harping with their harps" (Rev. 14:2).

And the last of a series of five doxologies closes the book of Psalms by admonishing us to praise God "with the sound of the trumpet . . . psaltery and harp . . . timbrel and dance . . . stringed instruments and organs . . . loud cymbals . . . Let everything that hath breath praise the Lord. Praise ye the Lord" (Ps. 150).

168. A general's philosophy

On his seventy-fifth birthday, General Douglas MacArthur said:

"Youth is not entirely a time of life; it is a state of mind. It is not wholly a matter of ripe cheeks, red lips, or supple knees. It is a temper of the will, a quality of the imagination, a vigor of the emotions . . . nobody grows old by merely living a number of years. People grow only by deserting their ideals.

"You are as young as your faith, as old as your doubt; as young as your self-confidence, as old as your fear; as young as your hope, as old as your despair.

"In the central place of every heart there is a recording chamber. So long as it receives a message of beauty, hope, cheer, and courage—so long are you young. When the wires are all down and your heart is covered with the snow of pessimism and the ice of cynicism, then, and only then, are you grown old."

169. What God is like

Some psychologists say children get their ideas about God from their fathers and their attitudes toward people from their mothers.

From earliest childhool, God is identified with maleness. "Our *Father* which art in heaven . . . ."

So if a child's father-thoughts are negative, he is likely to be turned off by the idea of God. Adult unbelievers almost always recall fathers who were cold, distant, stern, demanding, severe . . . and inevitably busy.

Charlie W. Shedd discusses this problem with keen insight on pages 69–71 of his book, *Promises to Peter.* He admits that no father can be perfect, and shows the importance of what he calls "contrast." Children must be taught to contrast what their fathers are to what God actually is. They must see that when their father is the right kind of daddy, that's how God is. But whenever their father fails in any role, they must see that God is the opposite. Otherwise they will grow up transferring all their father-feelings to God-feelings.

Shedd warns that the more "pious" the father (church-centered, Bible-carrying, moralistic) the more this distinction must be made clear.

170. Money-back guarantee?

Young people often come to the marriage altar with a fairy-story idealism. That is, they believe that once a person falls in love, he lives happily ever after! But unfortunately, there is no money-back guarantee in marriage. There is no proof of a happy ending. Marriages may be made in heaven, but they must be lived on earth.

A marriage license is something like a fishing license. It doesn't guarantee success; it just legalizes the try! Happiness is more likely when a bride and groom ask, "What can I *give* in this marriage?" rather than "What can I *get* from this marriage?"

An engaged couple was nearing their wedding day. The young man had a disfiguring scar from a childhood injury. Neither had mentioned the blemish. Thinking something should be said before they were married, he found the courage to ask his girl friend how she felt about it. She gave no answer, but simply reached over and kissed the scar. It was her way of saying that she accepted him as

he was, and that together they would build on life as it was, rather
than life as it might be.

171. Love vs. fear

In the summer of 1970, a coroner in London, England, ruled
that four-year-old Denise O'Connor died accidentally as a direct
result of her fear of a dentist. Dr. Gavin Thurton said that Denise's
heart stopped because of an excess of adrenalin in her bloodstream,
brought on by fear. Her parents testified at the inquest that they
and an anesthetist had tried twice to coax the girl into a dentist's
chair. Finally, Denise was then given a sedative, whereupon four
teeth were pulled. But minutes later, her heart stopped.

Bob Moore of Los Angeles, a lifeguard for thirty-five years, says
that guards spend their days handing out bandages, picking up
trash, or looking for lost objects, such as children, rings, watches,
and false teeth. "I'm afraid a lifeguard's job isn't what it's like in
the movies," he said in an interview. He pointed out that most
rescues usually occur in the shallows just off the beach. Victims are
people who start panicking when a wave hits them, and simply fall
face down. Gripped with fear, they can't get back up.

These two stories, both from real life, illustrate the deadly power
of fear. "I was almost scared to death" can be more truth than
fiction. Parents can be sympathetic with the hold that fear may have
on their children and seek ways to support them with their love and
assurance. Adults can seek to replace fear with love and trust,
recognizing the truth of 1 John 4:18, "There is no fear in love;
but perfect love casteth out fear." More is needed than merely
scolding a person not to be afraid. Fear must be replaced. The best
way to overcome fear is to crowd it out with love and trust. If
a person has no positive force such as love to replace fear, there
is no hope that his fear will be conquered. Because when one fear
is destroyed, another will rush in to fill the empty vacuum.

172. Ultimate decency

"I believe in an ultimate decency of things, and, if I woke up in
hell, I would still believe in it."—Robert Louis Stevenson.

173. "Take our heads out"

When the slave trade was thriving in West Africa, mercenaries would penetrate the interior to capture hundreds of natives. They would then clamp iron collars around their necks to keep them in check until they arrived back at the coast for shipment.

As the captives passed through other African villages on their way to the sea, a local chief or king would sometimes recognize a friend or relative. If he were financially able, and of a mind to, he could redeem his friend through payment of gold, silver, brass, or ivory. Out of this practice grew a slang word among the Bambara tribe of French West Africa which meant, "take his head out of the iron collar."

According to Eugene Nida in his book, *God's Word in Man's Language,* when the Bible was translated in the dialect of the Bambaras, a common word was sought for the abstract idea of redemption. The translator seized on the well-known phrase, "God took our heads out" to substitute for the word "redeem." So when the Bambara tribesmen read of God's redemption, they get the image of God sending his Son as payment to "take our heads out of the collar" of sin and death.

174. Breaking eggs

If you hold an egg too tightly, the shell will crumble and make a terrible mess in your hand. But if you hold an egg too lightly, it may drop to the floor and break.

The lowly egg has a message: Watch your grip on life—not too light, not too tight!

Take children, for example. Some parents keep such an iron-clad grip on their kids that they never learn to think for themselves. They slowly lose all originality, creativity, or curiosity for living. Other parents adopt a "hands off" attitude, only to see their children stumble and fall for lack of discipline, and the security that goes with discipline.

Money is another example. Keep too tight a hold on it and you become a miser. Spend it too freely and you are a profligate.

Your own personality is still another example. If you withdraw into a little world all your own, that world may be broken and crushed by your own narrowness. But if you release yourself too freely you may be labeled a do-gooder and an intruder in others' affairs.

The next time you pick up an egg, remember that with too firm a grip you break it; with too light a grip you drop it. Life is that way. Watch how you handle it!

175. Room for diversity

The next time you feel like making the world over in your own image, ask yourself the following questions:

What if there were only one color of the rainbow or of flowers? What if there were only one musical note on the keyboard, or one temperature on the thermostat? What if the wind blew in only one direction, or only one variety of vegetable grew in the garden?

What if there were only one menu at the table, or a single number in the telephone directory? What if everyone wore the same facial expression? What if the pharmacy sold only one drug? What if there were only one sign on the highway, and only one highway on the map? What if the Bible contained only one verse, and a year only one day?

Now aren't you glad that everyone doesn't see things exactly as you?

176. "Pick a Label"

Since 1960, the International Conference of Weekly Newspaper Editors has selected "The Golden Dozen," a collection of the best editorials appearing during the year in weekly newspapers.

The 1970 "Dozen," edited by Harry W. Stonecipher of Southern Illinois University, includes one by Mrs. M. J. Schneider entitled "Pick a Label." It originally appeared in the *Boyertown* (Pa.)

Times, and points out the danger of sticking labels on people we dislike. Here are selections:

There seems to be a deadly new game going round our country these days: "Pick a Label." It's as if we all have in our possession giant label-making machines and are convinced in the present crisis that each person needs a tag: radical, reactionary, establishment, hippie, square, pig, super-patriot, you name it.

Pick a label.

I have a son who has long hair and a mustache. He looks like what some people call a hippie. So what is a hippie? A drug addict, a person who doesn't work, a student trouble-maker, a traitor bent to destroy our country, a Black Panther, a "White Panther," a pink panther?

Pick a label.

I am a middle-aged mother and newspaper editor. I have tremendous respect for President Nixon and for the weight of the decisions he has to make. But I feel that no human being is infallible.

Pick a label.

It is easy when we meet someone who looks different, who talks different, who holds different views to pick up our label-maker, punch out a name and stick it on, completely obscuring that person's identity.

I found myself doing just that yesterday when I heard a man sounding off about how he would use his shotgun to chase off any "hippie" who tried to trespass on his land.

So easy to pick a label.

I appeal to all of us in these times of stress: Let us throw away our label-makers. They can be as deadly as guns.

For, having everyone carefully labeled, we can no longer see the persons behind the labels, the sons and neighbors we once knew. If their labels differ from ours, they become the enemy.

It is much easier to throw rocks or to shoot at labels than at people. Labels don't have fears or joys, hopes or needs. Only people have those.

Labels don't bleed when they die. Only people do that.

177. Forgiveness in Christ

In one of his books, Sam Shoemaker describes a young Roman Catholic student in Paris who went to confession in a casual manner that lacked any true indication of repentance.

The priest who listened was obviously a very wise person, because as penance he sent the youth to Notre Dame Cathedral to pray. "Near the altar on the right-hand side of the cathedral is a large crucifix mounted on the wall," he explained. "You are to get down on your knees in front of that cross, and recognizing it as a symbolic figure of the death of Christ, you are to say aloud, 'Jesus, you have done this for me, but I don't give a damn.' "

The boy agreed, and kneeling there in the cathedral he prayed, "Lord, you have done this for me." Then he repeated it, "Lord, you have done this for me . . ." But he couldn't bring himself to finish the proscribed sentence.

Finally, from the depths of a broken heart he cried, "Jesus, you have done this for me, and I do care."

178. Key to health

It is generally admitted that from one half to three fourths of all patients who visit a doctor have emotional, rather than physical, needs.

Dr. Richard Cabot, once a noted Christian physician in the Boston area, frequently asked a group of medical students, "Gentlemen, would you like to know the cause of almost every illness?" After a short dramatic pause, he answered his own question, *"It's the wear and tear of the soul upon the body."*

Voltaire recognized this decades ago when he wrote, "Doctors pour drugs of which they know little to cure diseases of which they know less, into human beings of whom they know nothing."

If we could understand the person, we could better understand his ailments.

Centuries ago, Plato wrote, "the great error of our day in the treatment of the human body is that physicians separate the soul from the body."

Yet many diseases are real, and the pain is not imagination. Even so, attitude is the key. As Theodore Farris said, "Health is precious, let nobody ever deny that, more precious than fine gold. But life is more than health and there are people who have not had good health who have had good lives, creative and wonderful beyond our imagination."

When he was president of Princeton University, Woodrow

Wilson suffered constantly. He prayed for healing, "not just for selfish reasons, but because I want to be the best university president possible." As the suffering continued, he changed his prayer, "Father, if the pain is not going to be taken *away,* then please give me the strength to *take* it." When God denied Paul's request for healing, he promised, "My grace is sufficient for thee: for my strength is made perfect in weakness" (2 Cor. 12:9).

179. Law of averages

During his amazing career, Babe Ruth hit a total of 714 home runs in regular games of big league baseball. What is less widely known is that he also struck out 1,330 times!

In an interview with Ruth, Grantland Rice asked him, "Babe, what do you do when you get in a batting slump?"

Babe replied: "I just keep goin' up there and keep swingin' at 'em. I know the old law of averages will hold good for me the same as it does for anybody else, if I keep havin' my healthy swings. If I strike out two or three times in a game or fail to get a hit for a week, why should I worry? Let the pitchers worry; they're the guys who're gonna suffer later on."

180. Where prayer starts

Marian Anderson, who has one of the most gifted voices ever heard by the American public, didn't just open her mouth and start singing. Success didn't come easy. As she says: "Failure and frustration are in the unwritten pages of everyone's record. I have had my share of them. We were poor folk, but many people were kind to me. A group of well-meaning friends hastily sponsored me for a concert in Town Hall in New York. But I wasn't ready, either in experience or maturity."

On the night of the concert, she was told the house was sold out. Waiting in dazed delight, her sponsor said there would be a slight delay. She waited five, ten, fifteen minutes. But as she peeked through the curtain, she saw the house was half empty. "I died inside," she said later.

"I sang my heart out, but when the concert was over I knew I had failed. The critics next day agreed with me. I was shattered within."

She told her mother she had best forget singing, who in return advised her to think about it a little and to pray about it a lot. But she was so crushed, that for a full year Marian Anderson refused all invitations to sing. Still her mother kept prodding: "Marian, have you prayed? Have you prayed?"

Marian admits that she didn't pray, but rather embraced her grief. Then there came a time when self-pity died, and she did pray. And one day she came home unaware that she was humming! It was her first effort in a whole year. Hearing her daughter's voice, Marian's mother rushed to meet her, then threw her arms about her as she kissed her. Then she added these words of advice to the black girl who was to become internationally famous, "Prayer begins where human capacity ends."

181. A Christmas prayer

O GOD our father, we are so busy this Christmas that unless we are careful, we will overlook thy gift. We are so rich that unless we give heed, we will disdain thy gift. We are so self-centered that unless we unthrone self, we will belittle thy gift.

THOU didst, in the long ago, hide thy Gift in Bethlehem. Only those who were humble, sought it. Only those who were seeking, found it. Only those who were unhurried saw it.

GRANT that we may rediscover thy Gift this Christmas. That is, may we find Him, and He be found in us. May we praise Him, and his loveliness be mirrored in us. May we serve Him, and his compassion be revealed in us.

AND IF—in thy mercy—thou dost choose to grant our wish, every day shall be Christmas, and every star an ornament, and every breath a paean of praise to thee. Amen.

182. Key to long life

George W. Gallup once made a study of 402 persons, each of whom was at least 95 years of age. He was looking for a key to their longevity, anxious to know what it was about these oldsters that kept them alive and functioning after many of their contemporaries were dead.

Gallup says he found one common trait: lack of tension, anxiety, and worry. Each was taking one day at a time. This does not mean these 402 individuals were somehow sheltered from the common problems of life, but they refused to let such anxieties tie them in knots.

One of those interviewed was William Perry, 106, who was then living in San Francisco. When he had a leg amputated at 102, doctors advised him to take a wheelchair. Three prosthetic suppliers refused to fit him with an artificial limb as "it would be a waste of money." In commenting on the incident, Perry said, "They told me to get a wheelchair, and I told them to go to hell. I learned to walk the first time a hundred years ago, and I could learn again." Which he did.

"There's no point in worrying" was the comment of Mrs. Marie Renier, 101, of Niles, Michigan. "All my life I cried when it was time to cry. I laughed when it was time to laugh, and I sang when it was time to sing."

183. He kept singing

Hymnwriter B. B. McKinney is remembered not only for such favorites as "Have Faith in God," "The Nail-Scarred Hand," and "Wherever He Leads I'll Go," but also for the fact that he liked to sing as well as to write music for others to sing.

During World War II, he was concerned for two sons in service. When someone questioned how he could sing during such dark days, he replied: "I sang before they left home; I am singing while they are gone; if they return I will sing; and if they don't return, I will still sing praises to my Lord."

For a number of summers, I enjoyed the music at Falls Creek Assembly in Oklahoma, led by Dr. McKinney. With a big smile he would say: "Now let's all sing. And if you don't, I'm going to send you to Sing Sing until you do sing!" That would do it. By then, everyone had reached for a hymnbook.

On Tuesday after Labor Day in 1952, Mrs. McKinney called her nephew, Porter W. Routh, in Nashville, Tennessee, saying they had been in an automobile accident at Soco Gap, North Carolina, on their way from Ridgecrest Baptist Assembly. Dr. McKinney was in serious condition in the new county hospital in Bryson City, North Carolina.

Routh flew to Knoxville, where he was met by Ramsey Pollard, who loaned him a car to drive over the Smokies to Bryson City. When he arrived about five in the afternoon, Routh met a young, redheaded doctor, perspiration streaming down his face. Just out of surgery, he said he had never been through such an experience.

"Dr. McKinney's blood pressure was about zero when we brought him in, and the first thing we wanted to do was give him blood to get over the initial shock. He was delirious. I have never been through such a choir practice. All the time we were trying to give him blood, he kept trying to get us to sing about Jesus."

A few days later, on September 7, the hymnwriter who got his initial inspiration from his mother who sang as she went about her household work, was dead. But the singing goes on!

184. Effortless success

Here's how to hit the bull's-eye every time! Fire at a blank target. Wherever the bullet strikes, select that spot as the bull's-eye and draw your concentric circles around it!

Absurd?

No more so than the aimless person who stumbles into one day after another, setting today's goal on the basis of yesterday's deed. Somewhat like saying that whatever is to be, will be. No risk, no sweat, no venture. Just sweet success, even though it is phony.

185. Long shadows

During the short days of winter when the sun hangs low in the south, a tree or a man or any object creates longer shadows on the ground.

This is also true near sunset, any season of the year. At sundown, a small boy makes a shadow as big as a giant. This phenomenon led someone to observe: "When little men start to cast long shadows, it is a sign that night is near."

There is more to this proverb than meets the eye, because the author is thinking not merely of an actual shadow cast by a short person. Rather he is thinking about influence and example.

Frequently a "little" person (in character, altruism, experience, morality, etc.) will carry more weight in a community than more mature persons. What he lacks in character he may make up for in cunningness, enthusiasm, and determination. And this is always a signal that darkness is coming. Not the actual blackness of night, but the darkness of prejudice and dishonesty and fraud and deceit.

This can also happen in a home, on the job, in a classroom, within the government, or even in a church. It occurs whenever the gifted and the virtuous sit back, while less-desirables take over.

186. Unpredictable behavior

It is frequently claimed that trouble brings out the best in people. But sometimes it brings out the worst.

When Hurricane Celia hit Corpus Christi, Texas, in the summer of 1970, a shortage of gasoline quickly led some dealers to jack the price from 32¢ to $1.59 a gallon. And during the resulting ice shortage, one iceman asked as high as $10 for a single 25-pound chunk.

Why is it that the same disaster may trigger courage in one person and cowardice in another? Or generosity and self-sacrifice in one and greed in another?

It is not the storm. The same high winds, lightning, floods, and hail strike all alike. The difference is in the person.

"The heart is deceitful above all things, and desperately wicked: who can know it?" (Jer. 17:9).

187. Home for Christmas

Sometimes we live so closely to history that we are blind to the most significant events. The trivial crowds out the monumental.

Orville and Wilbur Wright built a flying machine in their bicycle shop in Dayton, Ohio, and shipped it to Kitty Hawk, North Carolina, for trial flights because of the soft, sandy beaches in case of a crash.

There, on December 17, 1903, their plane, powered by an engine of their own design and make, rose of its own power, remained in the air 12 seconds, and covered a distance of 120 feet.

It was the first instance in human history of actual mechanical flight.

Yet the only report in the Dayton newspapers merely mentioned that the Wright brothers, who had been working on a flying machine in North Carolina, would be home for Christmas. One of the greatest news stories of the twentieth century was overlooked.

188. What counts

"The quality of leadership is the determining factor in every institution . . . . Whether it's the PTA, a country club, or a church, if you have the right person heading it up, it gets some place. If you don't, it doesn't. If you don't have leadership, you can appoint committees and draw organization charts and make speeches about cooperation until you're blue in the face, but nothing happens."—Cameron Hawley.

189. Half-truths

Half-truths can be more dangerous than outright lies, for a half-truth has enough validity to make it appealing to the naive and unthinking. Take some popular examples of half-truths:

"It pays to tithe." Yes, there are built-in values to tithing. But it is a falsehood to teach that if a person will just start to tithe on Sunday, he will strike an oil well in his backyard on Monday. Job, in the Old Testament, was a liberal giver, but he also suffered great losses. God blesses liberality, but his blessings do not always take the form of more dollars and cents.

"Families that pray together stay together." More than prayer is needed to hold a family together. The assumption is that a praying family will practice all the other admirable habits. But not necessarily so. Examples could be found of families that prayed every day, yet fell apart.

"Get on fire for the Lord, and folks will come to watch you burn up." The false emphasis here is on the preacher as a performer. Should crowds come to "watch the preacher burn up," or should they come to see the exalted Christ, shining through and over a dedicated prophet in the pulpit?

"Christ is the answer." True, Christ holds the answers for all of life's problems. But be careful of reducing the gospel to the level of the old-fashioned medicine show, which boasted of a tonic that could cure all ills. Beware of oversimplification, as if all one must do is walk down the aisle to accept Christ, and then live happily ever after! Problems do not end at the cross. For some converts, they start there. This is not denying that in Christ is the great Answer to all of life. It is simply saying that a glib, oversimplification of what it means to be a Christian can of itself be a half-truth.

"You either go forward or backwards. You can't stand still in the Christian life." Really? Moses said to Israel, "Fear ye not, stand still, and see the salvation of the Lord" (Ex. 14:13). Jahaziel said to Judah, "Ye shall not need to fight in this battle: set yourselves, stand ye still, and see the salvation of the Lord" (2 Chron. 20:17). And Ephesians 6:13 says, "Wherefore . . . having done all, to stand."

Christian spokesmen must not be content with half-truths. Jesus said, "And ye shall know the truth, and the truth shall make you free" (John 8:32). He didn't say "half-truths," for they make men only half-free.

190. In a box

A working mother enrolled her four-year-old daughter in a nursery school. Occasionally the director of the school would speak to the children or her helpers over the intercom. The children were always intrigued when her voice came out of the little box-like speaker.

After a few days, the mother asked her daughter if she had made any new friends. "Oh, yes," she answered, "and I like all my teachers but one."

"And who is she?"

"Oh, I don't know her name. You see, I haven't met her. She lives in a little box!"

We smile at her answer, but adults often make an even greater mistake in their concept of God. They visualize him as "up there in heaven" in some kind of a little box. But in reality, he is everywhere. Theologians use a big word to describe this part of God's nature. They call it omnipresence. It means he is everywhere at one time.

First Kings 8:27 states it this way, "Behold, the heaven and heaven of heavens cannot contain thee." God is too great to be fenced in. Yet some people try to box God in a church, or up in heaven, or in a Bible. Rather, we should say they *try* to. For to those who can sense his presence, he is all about.

191. Inspiration not enough

As pastor of the Trinity Baptist Church in San Antonio, Texas, Buckner Fanning led the congregation in a total outreach that ministered to the needs of people outside the walls of the church building. Juvenile delinquents, school dropouts, alcoholics, victims of accident and illness, homeless children—these were a few of the objects of their compassion.

Fanning tells of a conversation that really shook him up, that showed him lay people want to do more for Christ than listen to sermons.

He and a deacon from Trinity Church were returning from a retreat, one which Fanning felt was a real mountaintop experience. It had netted him numerous sermon ideas and notes for his preaching ministry. But when he asked the deacon for his reaction, he got an honest answer that shook him up.

"Yeah, Buckner, it was good," the deacon began. "But I want to tell you something. I've had all the inspiration I can stand.

I've taken my last note. I've remembered my last point. I've been importing, and I am satiated. I have been receiving. I have been taking in."

The deacon concluded by warning that unless his church could give him a handle whereby he could translate some of that inspiration into practical deeds of Christianity, he was through!

Merely inspiring the faithful without giving them an avenue of service is much like inflating the tires on a car that never goes anywhere. If a car stays parked in the garage all day, flat tires are just as good as inspired (inflated) tires!

192. People, too

Not only cars are recalled by their Maker.

193. Never crippled

During World War II, Harold Russell lost both hands in the blast of a TNT blockbuster. While in the hospital, a veteran of World War I visited him. He was a man by the name of Charley McGonegal, who likewise had lost both hands.

Harold Russell remembered one piece of advice which the older veteran gave him. "Remember, Harold, you are not crippled. You are merely handicapped."

Later, Mr. Russell compared the two words in a dictionary. Handicapped meant any disadvantage making success more difficult. But crippled meant incapable of effective action.

Every person is scarred in some way. If he considers himself a cripple, he will be disabled. But if he looks upon himself as only handicapped, he can still succeed even though success is now more difficult.

The difference is more likely in one's state of mind, rather than the severity of his wounds.

194. The little people

It was a big day in Aberdeen, South Dakota, when J. C. Penney visited the local Penney store, one of seventeen hundred in a chain. Local dignitaries, store officials, clerks, and newsmen cluttered around the entrance to greet the dedicated Christian layman who built his business on the Golden Rule. After an exchange of pleasantries, Mr. Penney happened to glance past the crowd and spotted a customer standing alone at a counter at the far end of the store. "And who," asked the master merchandiser, "is waiting on that lady back there?"

Self-styled pompous individuals are impressed with the crowds, the flashbulbs, and prominent people. But the really great people, and the great institutions, are interested in the little fellow, "the lady back there in the store," the visitor on the back pew.

In the midst of a great crowd, Jesus spotted and recognized a little man by the name of Zacchaeus, almost hidden in the branches of a tree.

The seeking, probing, searching nature of Christianity is explained in Luke 14:21: "Go out quickly into the streets and lanes of the city, and bring in hither the poor, and the maimed, and the halt, and the blind."

Or stated negatively, "I wept not, so of stone grew I within" (Dante).

195. Knowing Christ

In his foreword to *The New Testament in Modern English,* translator J. B. Phillips says that the letters of Paul "are alive, and they are moving . . . and their meaning can no more be appreciated by cold minute examination than can the beauty of a bird's flight be appreciated by dissection after its death." He feels it is meaningless "to study his writings microscopically, as it were, and deduce hidden meanings of which almost certainly he was unaware."

In this testimony, Phillips touches on a basic truth of the Christian faith—we do not prove Christ, but we experience him.

Nothing—education, power, wealth, logic—is to be compared with a personal experience. Christ is caught, not taught. We spread our faith like the measles—with personal contact.

Paul felt that this personal experience with Christ was so meaningful that as far as he was concerned, his proud position as a Benjaminite, as a Pharisee, as an Israelite, and as a Hebrew could be relegated to the dung heap, or garbage (see Phil. 3:5–8).

This does not mean that we run off in all directions at once, ecstatically crying, "Jesus only!" It does mean that he is our pearl of great price, the lily of the valley, the bright and morning star, the captain of our salvation, the head of the church, the light of the world, the prince of peace, the rose of Sharon, King of kings and Lord of Lords, whom to know aright is life everlasting.

196. One God for all

During the civil rights movement of the early 1960's, bombings were so common in Birmingham, Ala., that Negroes turned the city's official greeting around and said to one another, "It's nice to bomb you in Havingham." Before the Civil Rights Act of 1964 was passed, a dynamite charge killed four Negro girls at Sunday school in the Sixteenth Street Baptist Church in Birmingham.

Newsman Karl Fleming remembers finding a mimeographed church bulletin in the ruins of the church. On the cover was a picture of Jesus, his face crayoned black by some black child.

God is a Spirit, and thus has none of the human characteristics we identify with personality, such as color, race, height, etc. But Jesus was God incarnated in the flesh, and although he came with the racial characteristics of a Jew, everyone tends to identify Christ with himself. We see ourselves in him, and rightfully so, for he is all things to all men. No one has a monopoly on God. Whether we color him black or white, brown or yellow, he is the Father of all, and loves all as he loves each, and each as if there were none other to love.

"But to us there is but one God, the Father, of whom are all things, and we in him; and one Lord Jesus Christ, by whom are all things, and we by him" (1 Cor. 8:6).

"I will put my laws into their mind, and write them in their hearts: and I will be to them a God, and they shall be to me a people" (Heb. 8:10).

197. Constructive citizenship

"I hope to find my country in the right: however, I will stand by her, right or wrong." John J. Crittenden of Kentucky said this in a speech to the U.S. Congress in May, 1846, when President James K. Polk sent a message relating to war with Mexico.

But in a speech before the U.S. Senate in 1872, Carl Schurz of Missouri stated it this way, "Our country, right or wrong! When right, to be kept right; when wrong, to be put right!"

Writing in *The Defendant,* G. K. Chesterton warned that no patriot would say, "My country, right or wrong" except in a desperate case. He noted that it is like saying, "My mother, drunk or sober."

198. Weekday religion

It was her first visit to church, and the little girl was somewhat awed by the solemnity of the occasion. "Mama," she whispered during a brief pause in the service, "does the minister live here, or does he come down from heaven every Sunday?"

Our generation wants a "down here" religion in preference to one that is "up there." Unless the Christian faith can be translated into daily action, meeting the common needs of ordinary people, it is little more than a religion of superstition.

"Let Christ Jesus be your example as to what your attitude should be. For he, who had always been God by nature, did not cling to his prerogatives as God's equal, but stripped himself of all privilege by consenting to be a slave by nature and being born as mortal man" (Philippians 2:6–7, Phillips).

At the 1970 meeting of the Christian Booksellers Association, one spokesman said that in recent years the emphasis in religious books has shifted from such titles as "A Devotional Guide to

Serenity" to those such as "The Radical Suburb." Another publisher attributed some of this trend to a growing appreciation of what the martyred German theologian Dietrich Bonhoeffer called "the worldly interpretation" of Christianity, that is, not seeing Christianity as separate from the rest of life.

199. Builders or wreckers?

Napoleon Bonaparte wanted to be a writer, but the essays he submitted were laughed at. Adolf Hitler aspired to be a painter, but his work was rebuffed. Frustrated in their desires to be creative, both Hitler and Napoleon turned their energies toward destructiveness. Other examples can be found throughout history, because a basic human need is for creative self-expression. If this need is dammed up or diverted, it often expresses itself in the opposite direction. As Erich Fromm said, "The man who cannot create wants to destroy."

200. What leader?

Two tired donkeys approached a stream on a hot day. One was carrying a load of salt, and the other a huge pack of sponges. The first donkey, carrying salt, went down into the stream where the salt soon dissolved.

When he came out on the other side, he called back to his fellow donkey, saying what a marvelous experience he had as he lost his burden in the cooling stream.

Whereupon the second donkey plunged into the stream, but the sponges soaked up the water and caused him to drown.

Moral: Don't play "Follow the Leader" unless you have a fairly good idea where he's headed!